In the Long Room of Our Hearts:

WHERE LOVE AND MEMORY DWELL

ANN HEDGE-CARRUTHERS

BALBOA PRESS
A DIVISION OF HAY HOUSE

Balboa Press books may be ordered through booksellers or by contacting:

Balboa Press
A Division of Hay House
1663 Liberty Drive
Bloomington, IN 47403
www.balboapress.com
1 (877) 407-4847

Print information available on the last page.

ISBN: 978-1-9822-3043-2 (sc)
ISBN: 978-1-9822-3044-9 (hc)
ISBN: 978-1-9822-3048-7 (e)

Library of Congress Control Number: 2019908720

Balboa Press rev. date: 07/18/2019

This book is dedicated to

Our dear, loving girls: Rebecca, Bess, Melissa, Bailey,
Lizzy, Jayden, Aria, Zelda, and Jenny.

To Kim.

And to "T," who now walks in glory.

CONTENTS

A Word from the Author ix
Acknowledgments and Permissions xiii

Chapter 1 Won't You Please Go with Me? 1
Chapter 2 The Rocking Chair and The Teapot 4
Chapter 3 The Crayolas and The Coloring Book 17
Chapter 4 The Dancer 25
Chapter 5 The Flint, The Preacher, and The Fool 33
Chapter 6 The Hill Country 43
Chapter 7 The Milagros 52
Chapter 8 The Sabbatical 61
Chapter 9 The Poverty of Desire 74
Chapter 10 The Rings 85
Chapter 11 The Fireworks 89
Chapter 12 The Frog 97
Chapter 13 The Dictionaries 102
Chapter 14 The Sad Little Clock 107
Chapter 15 The Letters 113
Chapter 16 The Cassock 122
Chapter 17 The Walnut Box 127
Chapter 18 The Vow 138
Chapter 19 The Mystical Stairway 142
Chapter 20 The Bumper Sticker 150
Chapter 21 The Stones 164
Chapter 22 The Fears 168
Chapter 23 The Watch, The Note, and The Fish Crows 172

Endnotes 179

A WORD FROM THE AUTHOR

After reading this book, my friend Meta Gustafson asked me two questions that may be raised by my reader. The first is, Why was the book written? What is its purpose and method? The second is, What exactly do I want my reader to get from the book?

After Bob passed from my sight, I simply could not recover from the loss. I sought counseling, but I could not get past a certain point, so I began to write. Eventually, things began to fall into place. Grief never goes away; its claws dig in too deep. But it does not have to be the focus of one's life, as it had become in mine. I felt as if the project of writing became one that Bob and I shared. It was a joy, and when the last words were written, I felt both grateful to have done it and sorry that it could not go on and on.

Initially, my attempts at a biography of Bob's life proved fruitless. But I continued to write artlessly. I was relying on old records and letters, newspaper clippings, photographs, and the tales that Bob had told me as well as those recorded by Bob's friends when I feared his complete loss of memory. It was a great way to occupy myself in the dark, dumb days, but it was pathetic writing. Finally, a friend and former classmate of mine, Kim Bateman, asked me why I did not write in my own style. I asked her what that style was! She reminded me of things I had written twenty or more years before. She told me to write about memories just as I always had. That was my style—memories, lively memories that swirl about themselves with no mind given to time, old and more recent memories twisting about themselves as if dancing a reel. She waved her arm about my living room as she said, "I bet there are enough memories found in the objects in this room to fill countless books." Suddenly the writing began to flow freely.

Some have chronological, tidy memories, but mine are a mass of thoughts and feelings. Sometimes I find that they come so fast and disorderly that if

I could write two or more things at once, I could more nearly capture what is going on within—happy, sad, joyous, longing, and always grateful as they tumble out.

There will be times when my reader will not know if they are reading about older events or more recent ones. I find that what happens today pulls at the strings of yesterday. When Meta said that she could not tell if I was speaking about things old or more nearly new, I was not surprised. Can a memory be old if it is working on my psyche in the present? How can it be old if the emotions it stirs and the images created are happening as I write? This is not an autobiography. It is not even a memoir. It is a *disorderly collection of memories*. Each chapter is its own, belonging to no other and mostly without order. So I ask my reader not to expect anything chronological here. Just let the story flow, and if you get lost, read faster. If there is any order here, it is in the disorder.

As for Meta's second question, the book finds its roots in a conversation with Bob's most recent editor, Rob Slocum, who suggested that if I wrapped some of Bob's poems in a narrative, the poems would be more marketable. The hardest part of writing has been choosing which poems to use and which to leave out. Some of the most appealing poems just hang out there in a copyright limbo because the journals are no longer published and the organizations behind them are not organized, so there is no way to acquire copyright information or permission. Also, knowing that I am writing for people who have not picked up a book looking for poems has required me to use some of the more straightforward poems.

In all instances, I have tried to frame each poem in ways that will make their meaning more accessible and help tell parts of the story. I plead with you to read these poems. Read them for their beauty of metaphor and the flow of words. Meaning may come, and it may not. But the meaning is not the issue; the images are. Images are the language of the soul, and they take you straight to the heart of the poet. Don't fall back on the old belief that you can't read poetry; that was in high school when few of us had a mind for it.

My third reason for writing is to show how darkness opened onto light, time and again. The saddest and most disappointing of events become the seeds of healthy growth and maturity. In those times when we or others would have done great harm, willfully or not, the Almighty takes hold of it and tortures it into the shape of goodness. The Divine will not be outdone.

I was assisted by Brandon Middleton, LLD, in complying with copyright law. I also want to thank him for his encouragement. I was supported all along by Bobby Reynolds, Linnie Lyle, and Linda Austin. Bobby read one of the earlier drafts, and that is a true act of love. These are all strong, loving women who have lent me their fortitude.

I also should acknowledge the excellent mixer of martinis, John, who along with Sharon listened to my unending complaints about the pains and exasperations of getting the details finished up.

More than seventy people who were friends of Bob's and mine took the time to sign notarized letters giving me permission to use their names or refer to them. I realize the nuisance and inconvenience of this, and I am beholden to each of you.

I also want to recognize the loving hands and hearts of Regina Washington, Jan Smith, and Joyce Perry, who helped me care for Bob. You know that I could never have cared for him so well all on my own. I am forever indebted to you. We shared laughter and tears and became family.

I have also been blessed with neighbors who have watched over me. Tim Guffey and Victor Puleo have kept close tabs on me through all of this. I act as if that is unnecessary, but I love the attention and likely need it too. They have introduced me to wonderful new friends, all coaxing me out of grief. Dick and Nancy Horne saw to it that I did not fall behind on my fried catfish quota in Bob's absence. Now, Dick too has moved beyond our sight, so Nancy and I muddle along.

Trinity Cathedral played an enormous role in my recovery. My friends there are considerable in number and it is far beyond my ability to call them each by name; but they must know who they are, unless they think that I am referring to some grand gesture and not considering the small kindnesses. (No kindness is small to the grieving.) These dear people, clergy and laity, have helped to hold my soul in the cleft of the Rock while the storm passed.

My profound gratitude to all of you.

Little Rock
Spring 2017

ACKNOWLEDGMENTS AND PERMISSIONS

In addition to all those whom I have expressed gratitude to in the preface, I wish to also thank the following:

The Anglican Theological Review Board and Jackie Winter, in particular, who gave me carte blanch to use poetry that Robert Cooper had published over the years.

John Herndon, who gave permission to reprint "An Ships and An Ocean" by Robert Cooper from *Periplum: An Anthology of Austin Poets,* published by Open Theater Publications, © 1987.

The Christian Century: An Ecumenical Weekly, for permission to reprint "Everything Died Today," by Robert Cooper, in no. 89, published August 28, 1972.

David Craig and Janet McCann, editors, and the Department of English at Texas A&M for use of *Odd Angles of Heaven: Contemporary Poetry of People of Faith,* by Robert Cooper. Published in 1998.

The Episcopal Diocese of Tennessee, the Rt. Rev. John C. Bauerschmidt, bishop of the Diocese of Tennessee, for permission to use "Laying on of Hands" by Robert Cooper published in *The Tennessee Churchman,* © 1971.

The American Classical League for permission to use the poems "Patmos" and "Panther," by Robert Cooper published in *The Classical Outlook* 75.1 of 1997.

The Jackson Writer's Group, publishers of *Old Hickory Review,* By Robert Cooper © expired.

The C. G. Jung Institute of Los Angeles for publication of "Pangea" by Robert Cooper and published in *Psychological Perspectives* 38, winter issue, 1998–1999.

The Living Church for their kind assistance in the reprinting of "Propers for an Unfixed Holy Day" by Robert Cooper, published in Edition 182, no. 4, January 25, 1981).

The Seminary of the Southwest for permission to reprint "St. Bruno" by Robert Cooper from *Ratherview,* edited by Anne Hoey, 1982.

Seabury Press for their assistance in the use of "Say When the Dying is Done" by Robert Cooper in *Imagination and Ministry,* authored by Urban T. Holmes.

Liveright Press for permission to print excerpts from "i carry your heart within me" by e. e. cummings in *E. E. Cummings Complete Poems 1904–1962,* edited by George J. Firmage (New York: Liveright Publishing Corporation, 1991).

Princeton Press for permission to quote from Either/Or by S. Kierkegaard, translated by Howard V. Hong and Edna H. Hong, © 1987.

Linda Ori for permission to print "!The Frog," published on her page at PoemHunters.com, 2007.

W. W. Norton for permission to print excerpts from "The Second Elegy in Dunio Elegies," written by Renier Maria Rilke translated by J. B. Leishmann and Stephen Spender, © 1963.

Robert Blak Slocum, who edited *Engaging the Spirit: Essays on the Life and Theology of the Holy Spirit* and *A Heart for the Future,* and who gave permission to reprint excerpts from the essays by Robert M. Cooper, "The Spirite Searcheth the Bottom of Goddess Secrets" and "This Body of Hope," and both published by Seabury Press, © 2001, and rereleased by Wipt & Stock Publishing, Inc., 2017.

The events and conversations recorded here are written to the best of the author's recollection. Some details have been changed to protect the privacy of individuals.

The term "seemingly unpublished" is used to indicate those poems that the author believed to be unpublished. The method used was to first catalogue all publications Ann Hedge-Carruthers had in her possession that included the works published under the names of Robert Cooper and Robert M. Cooper. From this catalogue, publishers were located. If a source was still unknown, the journals in which he had published most often were contacted. These journals have no system for cross-referencing poetry. If an error has occurred, it was only after due diligence was made, and the author will do what she can to correct all errors of attribution. This effort to correct errors extends to all other attributed or unattributed sources.

CHAPTER 1

Won't You Please Go with Me?

Love is not love
Which alters when it alteration finds …
But bears it out even to the edge of doom.

—William Shakespeare, "Sonnet 116"

It was one of those cold, crystal-clear mornings that are not uncommon to February in Arkansas. There had been room for only one passenger, and I wanted to be as close to Bob for as long as I could, so my sister, Sharon, drove along behind. Time and again, Bob had pled with me to go with him, and I had promised that I would go as far as I could and stay until someone came who knew the rest of the way. I had been his interpreter of the world for a long time now, and he could not imagine finding his way without me. My promises would quiet him but not necessarily satisfy him. He did not want to be separated from me—nor I from him.

We, the driver and I, rode in silence to a tiny country town where the crematorium was located, about an hour's drive north of Little Rock. I cannot tell you exactly what was running through my mind as we drove along. Mostly I remember looking at my hands, idle, red, chapped—hands scrubbed sore and at the same time graced by the incongruity of a diamond-encrusted band, now captured in the light of the sun. I must have been recalling the day we bought my beautiful wedding ring, the happiness and excitement of the moment. I had never grown tired of it or my life with Bob. It was love that had brought me to this place on this frigid morning, and yet there was no sense of life within me at all. My heart was no longer my own. I had given it to another, and it had now passed away. In its place was the heart of one whom I could no longer touch or see. We had often quoted e. e. cummings to each other. One lover saying to the other that his or her heart belonged to the other, "i carry your heart with me (i carry it/ in my heart) i am never without it (anywhere/ i go you go …"[1]

It is a beautiful poem, but on this morning, it had become so horribly real. A piece of me was missing and gone, so far away. If I had a heart that was his and it hurt so badly, then how did he feel? My thoughts were racing out far ahead of me. I would, in the months to follow, struggle to be all right so that Bob could be too. I eventually would come to my senses and realize that that was beyond my control and that I would be well again in whatever time it took to be well; self-condemnation would only make things worse.

When we arrived at the funeral home, Sharon and I were escorted to the lobby, and after a short wait, a man approached from the rear hallway. He asked that we follow him out to another much cruder building—to the furnace. Bob's body was there waiting. I stepped to him, and placing my left hand on his chest and my right on his head, I kissed him, or rather I kissed his beautiful, alabaster form, for the last time and told him again that I loved him. When I straightened, they slid his body forward toward the flames. I could see them blazing before me and feel their heat. In that moment, I knew nothing of soul or spirit. I was all body, and I was being torn from life. Bone being cracked away from bone and flesh torn from flesh. It was as if a wild beast had entered the arena. If the angels had come to show him the way, I could only hope. I had no sense of their presence, only the pain of longing and my life's greatest loss. What I did have was the comfort of the presence of my sister who hovered nearby. We were shown to her car. I asked her to drive around the building so that I could see the heat as it rose up from the chimney. We watched a while, and then with great reluctance, I allowed myself to be driven away. The poet of the "Song of Solomon" said, and it is true, love is as strong as death. Death had done its worst, but love remained. I can truly say that I loved Bob more the day he died than I loved him in the height of passion in those early days.

What a wonderful, exciting, curious, joy-filled, and sometimes excruciatingly painful way love had brought us, Bob and me. But I had had something that many never have a chance at having. I have been adored by a man whom I have adored in return. He was my teacher, my mentor, my friend, my lover, my delight, my soul mate—the love of my life. The person who stood at that furnace door was a person who largely had been shaped by her life with him. All of that is inviolate and abides somewhere untouched by flames, or physical absence, or grief. What is a catastrophic illness and death in the face of such a gift as that? My story is one of gratitude, though it is at times filled with sorrow. When grief comes to bury and destroy, gratitude and love will have none of it.

The work of the eyes is done now,
Go and do the heart-work
on the images imprisoned within you ...

—Rainer Maria Rilke, "Turning Point"[2]

CHAPTER 2

The Rocking Chair and The Teapot

And if, as toward the silent tomb we go
Though love, through hope and faith's transcendent dower
We feel that we are greater than we know.

—William Wordsworth, "Valedictory Sonnet to the River Duddon"

The rocking chair had been in Bob's office at the seminary when we first met. I had sat in it for hours. In that chair, I had drunk gallons of tea that he had brewed on a hot plate on the window ledge. First, Bob was my academic advisor, and later my professor. Through all of this, we became friends, and as graduation neared, we became more and more grim about how a friendship could continue once we were separated, with both of us involved in demanding jobs. We would likely drift away, and that was unbearably sad. That last spring, we had begun having lunch together. It was now just weeks before my graduation. I would be leaving soon, and we were trying to cram in as much time together as we could. I brought cheese, and he a banana, and there was always tea. All of the classes that he taught me were long past, so all we had before us was the exchange of ideas and talk about things we were reading—and about the state of our own souls.

We had always talked about life and school, about the joy and the spirituality we had both experienced in the process of studying; we knew it could open onto a mystical experience. This was not the first time we had spoken of this, but it was on my mind again with my classes ending and my return to full-time parochial work. Years before, Bob had suggested that I read Pascal, as he had with many of his students. I saw it spelled out in a way more eloquently than I had been able to describe it for myself; the Almighty was in the learning for Pascal. Often Bob would read to me what he was writing, and I read my short stories to him. He called them vignettes; I thought the term dismissive. Now here I am writing them again—vignettes—just brief and fleeting memories. We talked about our childhoods and marveled at how similar these had been, though we had been half a continent and almost ten years apart. Our fathers were not necessarily polished men, but our mothers were refined. I knew Bob in both ways. Both parents were alive in him, as mine were in me.

Initially, Bob and I had had an important but significant conversation in his office when he was assigned as my academic advisor. He struck me as a courtly southern gentleman who rose at my entrance. His voice was that North Carolina kind of soft, though he was never soft-spoken—God no! But being in his office was no preparation for being in his classroom. His classes were like a wild bronco ride. His language was more colorful than I had ever heard before, from him anyway. I must admit that at times I thought I had wandered into an agricultural class, given the references to what could have been excrement mucked from the barn. But propriety was not necessarily something in which Bob was interested. He was interested in the genuine, and the preciousness rampant among some clergy was disgusting to him. If he had to shock it out of his students, he never hesitated. I have been told by students whom he had taught previously, in the days when he was preparing only men for ordination, that he once said, "Boys, if you want to warm your butts at the fires of truth, be sure you don't have paper assholes."

There was nothing ornate or "churchified" about the classrooms where I attended lectures. At the front of the rooms were library tables, and on those rested simple lecterns. Bob's legs were so long that he could stand on one foot and put the other on the tabletop. From this raised knee, he then levered his pipe back and forth to his mouth. Only when he would stop to relight it could we students catch our own breaths in preparation for the next onslaught. He was wonderful, dazzling even, pulling bits and pieces from everywhere to make a point. First it was Plato, then Aristotle or the Bible and Kierkegaard, always Kierkegaard and St. Augustine of Hippo. It was never surprising for him to pull a clipping from the *New York Times* out of his shirt pocket and use that to make what we were talking about relevant to our own time. Greek and Hebrew and Latin were all whirled together. There was Dante and Shakespeare, all of it coming so unbelievably fast. This was another side of Bob that I had not seen in the quietness of his office where conversation was slow and drawn out, savored. Bob was the most complex and fascinating man I have ever encountered, both exquisitely lovely and delightfully naughty.

The habit of reading to each other that had begun in his office would become a significant part of our life together over the years. We would spend evenings reading, either in bed or on the sofa, with the feet of the listener in the lap of the reader, an arrangement that worked far better when he was reading. His size 13 feet would push the book up to my nose! Alternately, he would choose a book, and then I chose. He read beautifully, far more lyrically than I. Then one rainy weekend, I chose a book that was touching to me. I had read it several times, but even though I knew it well, I ultimately could not read for the tears that were blurring my vision. Bob took the book, finished it for me, and from that point forward, he did the reading as he sipped some George Dickel or Bombay Sapphire to ease his throat. This was not a nightly thing, but when we found something we thought we would both enjoy, we read; rather, he read. This was not all fiction; nonfiction was a frequent choice, and biographical works made their way onto the list occasionally—and of course poetry, always poetry. I recall one lovely, early-summer weekend when we read Mary Stuart's *The Crystal Cave,* sitting first on the balcony in the cool morning breeze and moving inside as the day warmed. There were so many others, books and times, that I cannot recall them all with any detail. The last book Bob read to me was one written by John Bayley, a memoir of the last years with his wife, Iris Murdock, philosopher and novelist. Bayley wrote of their passionate love affair, of her brilliance, their life together teaching at Oxford, and, ultimately, her descent into Alzheimer's disease. It is a tragic book, and I wept as Bob read. And because I already knew that something was terribly amiss, I felt the chill of premonition coming over me.

We came to Little Rock because Bob had a part to play at Trinity Cathedral. And he had far more of an impact there than I knew about until after his death. His last years in ministry were in a small mission with few communicants—few but dedicated and loving. Little Rock is a small southern city and is, like other cities in the South, hard to make one's way into. We had not had time for it to become our home before Bob's illness made it harder for him to socialize. I was in a profession that was isolating, as was the demand of tending to him. I had dreaded a small funeral in a large church. I had visions of us rattling around in there. For these reasons, I was astonished at how many people attended the service. In the years before Bob's death, I obsessed about where home was. I could not think of anywhere that was home if it did not contain Bob. For this reason as much as any other, Bob's body was cremated so that I could keep his ashes with me. He knew that this would be our plan, and he was relieved by it.

Bob was terrified of being left alone and had said over and over again that he wanted my ashes comingled with his and those of precious-dog-Charlie—he never failed to mention Charlie. He almost obsessed about this. Of course, I cannot do that. I cannot mingle our ashes. I can only hope that others will understand how important it was to him—and to me. But where those ashes will finally come to rest, I do not know. I have made friends here now, and it would not be a bad place to be. But there are other places too, and I cannot know where I will ultimately settle. Circumstances carry far more weight than our choices.

Bob also came to fear being left alone in life as well. My mother had died young, well youngish, and I, my confidence having played out, prayed that I would live long enough to see Bob to his end. Now his ashes are here beside me on the bedroom hearth, and between us lies Charlie, warming his aging bones by the fire. We are becoming the ancestors, sitting here awaiting the coming of Hestia, goddess of the hearth and the ashes of the ancestors buried beneath it; soon she will be coming to tend to us as we three sit and wait by the fire.

January

When I was king of Lithuania
I would sit by the fireplace in winter

> The cigar smoke went up the chimney
> I imagined that it blew all the way
> to Latvia so in a moment now
> in the doorway the way you can sometimes
> glimpse at evening a form move at the crossing
> streets you think you recognize It is only
> a woman or a man only that or smoke
> from the neighbor's burning and your eyes
> your eyes are older than their head's body
> In the southwestern sky you look for the comet
> the long smudge the blur of it your child's
> indelible faded mark on the nursery wall
> It can't be you think you really saw it
> but then you were the king of Lithuania
> and your eyes are always regal you saw the apple
> fall before Isaac did you fathom the gases
> the dust and you feel yourself settle things again
> settle into the hearth in your kingdom
> where ice and fire can be one thing as they were once
> when all this began and you alone knew
> the way to the sea and the way back again.
> (Cooper)[3]

Fairly early on, Bob had told me that he thought it best to get things out in the open so that they could not work on us at an unconscious level. He said he found me quite attractive and that he sometimes "found his motor running." I was stunned and flattered, but he was the expert, and if he said that he could just dust his hands of it and move on, I believed him; and for years, it had worked. Also, I was under the misconception that he was far older than I, and that made him not only the expert but far beyond the reach of my vulnerabilities. I never took it for granted that I was the only woman to whom he had said this. There were many women in his life, and he never hesitated to mention them; there was nothing coy about it, no pretending to keep secrets. It was always right out there and apropos of the conversations in which these women were mentioned. Not long after his death, I found his journals in the attic. They spanned roughly twenty-five years, beginning in his mid to late twenties. I found little there that he had not told me over the years, but something new was a list of those he considered his confidants, a list he had compiled in the early eighties. Even with all these years passed, I was still thrilled to find my name at the top of that list. There were seven names in all. Five were women, two of those ordained colleagues who lived at a distance; the remaining women were classmates of mine, and two were men, nonstudents, one a psychologist and the other a psychiatrist. Aside from his colleagues, we were all people he had come to know since his arrival at the seminary not long before.

I believe that he was sound as a confidant, always keeping a professional distance, until he was turned down for the deanship of the seminary and, at age fifty, gave up the sense that he had to press himself ahead professionally for the sake of friends and family who had high expectations of him. Toward the end of the journals when his entries become increasingly sparse, he speaks of having a sense of obligation to be dean because he did not want to disappoint others. He had never wanted to be dean, it seems; it was duty and responsibility that had pushed him ahead. What he would later write was that it was this failure that had set him free from this bondage to duty. In the journal entry dated 8-25-86 he wrote:

> When I gave up—finally—wanting to be a dean, (or when I was finally given up on by any who might want me to be dean—including my ... colleagues) something was released in me. If I see this at all clearly, and maybe I do see it more clearly now, that last time ... was of extreme importance.
>
> 1. I began to get free of the expectations that others had of me, expectations that were either actually there or where I had placed them upon myself. I began to give up partially
>
> on duty
> obligation
> making things right
> doing right
> being perfect
>
> This seems so to me now by hindsight. But mainly, I gave up on trying to do something that *I really did not want to do,*

> something that I could do—and do well—but in my heart did not really want to do. There is now some self-loathing about that factor in my character. I am, however, grateful for release.
>
> 2. To what extent am I to consider that as a preliminary step to moving out/on? [here he mentions making major changes] I feel/think that it was such a preliminary ... at this distance it feels like it was ...
>
> I don't have to do something that I really did not want to do. I don't have to try to be perfect.

But this was a slow and painful process for him, and it would take time to bear fruit. I watched it happen from a certain distance but did not always know what was going on with any exactitude. Following this rejection as dean, he was given a sabbatical, and when he returned, it was my senior year. He had begun to laugh more easily; he was more flexible and easygoing in his manner. Something was more relaxed about him, and he spoke of himself more readily—his hopes and fears. (Bob was the first man I had ever known who spoke of his fears, and I did not always like it. Over my lifetime, men had told me not to be silly, that all was well, and I had made use of that and treated it as if their words were reality. But with Bob, there was no pretending; he owned his fears, which meant that I could not take shelter in some false reality.) It was the latter, the free, almost reckless talk of himself, that destroyed the carefully constructed wall that we had built between ourselves—the wall that I had so keenly relied upon. It was built almost entirely on his well-tended aloofness and reticence to speak of personal of matters that concerned him deeply. I had always had the freedom to speak of anything I chose; now he had begun to do the same—slowly, slowly at first but increasingly over the following months. After my graduation and with the passing of his fiftieth birthday, the dam simply broke.

I don't mean to imply that I was oblivious of him before this. He was a charismatic man, powerfully sexual beneath his priestly vows. A woman whom he admired greatly and who was one of the two priests on his list of confidants had asked him once what he did with all the women who had fallen in love with him. I, on the other hand, had no sense of being handled or seduced—never, even though he had been open and inviting. Frequently there were notes in my box or on my carrel asking me to stop by his office for tea. But that he had seduced me was his great fear—that he had harmed me, that he had pulled me into what he saw as the nastiness of his life. I suspected this was his fear because he spoke of it when referring to Kierkegaard. Decades later, I found note of it in the journal entries that come from that period of dark moods. His journals are filled with this fear that he was sucking me into the maelstrom of his psyche. I guess in some way he had, but my psyche was a mess too. My advantage in the undoing of my life was that it had been much cleaner, uncomplicated, and understood by those who truly knew me.

Bob journaled less and less and then suddenly stopped entirely. That habit of nearly twenty-five years evaporated with one brief comment on how he had failed to do it regularly. It is written with a possible tone of self-recrimination, but I suppose that the journaling was one of those things that he had found that he "did not have to do."

The finding of Bob's journals has been a gift to me. If he had spoken of them, I had not understood the number of them or depth of pain reported in them. There is in them almost nothing, no event that he had not spoken of in our conversations over the years, but he had never quite managed to communicate in their intensity the emotions written of there. Perhaps time had scrubbed some of the feelings from his memory; I can't know. At any rate, these events of the past were written with such a profundity of sorrow that he had been unable to repeat years later in conversation. He also wrote of books he was reading and the thoughts that these had provoked. The books are still on our shelves, and I have read many simply because they appear in his journals. It is our book club, his and mine. I read as he read and then see what he was thinking. In addition to events and books, he reports dreams. For one such as I, who interprets dreams for my patients, these dreams are powerful insights into the depths of his psyche. We had shared our dreams over the years, and they are there in the journals, but there are also the dreams of the years before we met as well.

Over the years, Bob and I had grown accustomed to expressing our thoughts to each other. Sometimes these were so oblique that we would have to put them in writing to create enough clarity to express them. We are both convoluted people and could never know the whole of ourselves, much less that of the other. But we had undertaken the exploration of our psyches together and for a considerable number of years. We had been friends eight, almost nine, years before we married, and because of that, we were never disillusioned, one by the other. And oh, how I loved what I got, and I got what I loved. I knew he would say the same; I did not expect to change him. We were flawed, and we were damaged. We had harmed ourselves and others, but love had cushioned us from all that as we worked things through. Before we married, I made a list of the things about him that could annoy me and asked myself if there was anything or any combination of things on that list that was insurmountable. When the list was written, I laughed out loud. I think I still have it stuffed in a portfolio around here somewhere, and it still amused me the last time I read it. Aside from his intellect and lack of inhibitions, I was drawn to him because of his height and broad shoulders. I'm still a sucker for tall, powerful men; my daddy was one of those, if slighter in build. One day Bob asked me to describe "yo' Papa" as he put it. As I described my father, I was describing Bob. I blushed with embarrassment. I thought to myself as I studied the floor, *My God, I have fallen in love with my father.* Freud had won again!

Bob's nose was hooked like Papa's, though Papa never wore aviator glasses on his. Both men had brown eyes, but Bob's were piercing, close-set eyes. All of this added up to a stern-looking man—until Bob broke into a smile, and then the dimples took over his face. He also had a wonderful laugh, and I found him to be a funny man with a quick and sometimes biting wit. Someone, a longtime acquaintance of Bob's, recently described him as having a "wicked wit," and they were right. Politicians, DJs, journalists, and the clergy came in for the roughest treatment from him. He said that when they died, they would all have to listen to everything they had ever said recorded on perpetually playing tapes. Of course the first likely gatherings for him to say this to were clergy conferences where he was the speaker and seminary classes. Come to think of it, he said it to just about any group where he thought it was time for a little comic relief. When I first knew him, he was both conservative and liberal; he was forceful and almost overwhelming in his opinions. He was incensed by injustice and could waste the earth to bring it to an end. People had said that they were afraid of him, something that hurt him deeply because more than anything he craved the closeness of friendships. I was never afraid of him; perhaps because my father was a powerfully emotional man, and early on I had had to learn to stand my ground with him. I had had some practice at holding my own with powerful men. I think that in some important ways, I won Bob over to my thinking. I'm sure I did; it was not a one-sided relationship. I think that was when we learned to fight the right way, until illness had overtaken him and he was no longer able to reason in a calm way. (I almost said dispassionate, but I don't think that Bob was ever dispassionate; he seemed to care about everything.) We stated our cases, forcefully at times, and either found the other's point of view to be more reasonable than our own, or we found a compromise, or we decided to forget about it and just be lovers. I think that Will Spong taught us that; he would say there is just not enough time left to be angry. Then there were times when we just had screaming fits. I don't mean to overstate the case for compatibility; passion is passion, and it can be found in a lot of places, not just in bed—and not always under the control of grace. Indifference was something that neither of us knew much about.

Recently I was looking out the kitchen windows and marveling at the beauty of the white Carolina jasmine that have grown up, covering the west garden wall. It is spring now, and the flowers are profuse. They smell like gardenias. As I stood there, a smile came across my face and then laughter; memory had taken me over once again. Soon after we moved here, I had spent days on end working in that space, getting the ground cover in all along that side of the house and under the wall. Then I had dug holes for the roses and begun the process of training them upward. The jasmine was placed to grow up the lattice as well. Last, I had put down pavers. At this point, Bob came sauntering around the corner of the house. Pulling gloves on his hands, he began telling me what I should have done and how to redo it. (I was mud covered with sweaty hair stinging my eyes and a considerable sense of smugness at the accomplishment of a job well done.) His advice did not go down well with me, and we had a true conflagration of an argument over whose yard it was. Oh my! We could laugh and love together, we could write and read to and for each other, we could enjoy friends and travel and teach classes together. We could do every other kind of thing together with enormous delight, but we could not work around the house together. It always ended the same way; he would show up when it was just about time for applause and start telling me how to make things better. And no kitchen was ever large enough for the two of us. Now he might tell the tale differently, but I doubt it. I think that a sly smile of recognition would spread across his face were he reading this, and we would end in laughter.

But then telling tales is not a domestic enterprise. It was the domestic stuff of life where we ran off the rails. Well, that is not entirely true. Bob liked to think of himself as a feminist, and he took pride in pushing the vacuum about the center of rooms. You can't fault someone for trying; so the corners were done when he was out of the house. That was likely a run to the grocery store because he loved doing that. And nobody was better at loading a dishwasher or packing a box than he. How I miss him! When our dear friend Ernest Bel died, Joanie, who loved him deeply, stepped away from her grief for a moment of lightheartedness when she said to me, "Now I'll have to go to the grocery store." For a long time, Joyce, Bob's aide, made the weekly trips to do the shopping. Now I'm in the same fix as Joanie. Sometimes I think I would rather starve than shop. First of all, I just don't like the task; second, they play that music that takes me back to our happy times and leaves me feeling melancholy. Dante, in the *Divine Comedy*, placed words in Francesca's mouth to the effect that there is nothing more sorrowful than to remember happy times in the midst of sadness. I don't know if that is always true, but it certainly is when one is in the grocery store!

Bob and I enjoyed sharpening our wits against each other—in the healthy years. I can't recall a time when we did this in an antagonistic way but rather in an open and forthright one and usually for fun. I was never made to feel inferior to him. I don't think that ever occurred to him; we admired each other. But over time, this professional relationship gave way to friendship that then opened onto our affection for each other. Eventually we found ourselves to be deeply in love but not with a misty-eyed miscomprehension of each other. Our eyes were wide open. (Ah! How Zen of me to say that; Bob would have been pleased.) I knew who he was, and he knew me—or perhaps I should say that we knew as much of each other as it is possible to know. I did have an apprehension, however, that the imbalance in our stations in life might exist in an occult way, so I insisted that, once we were married, we would go into counseling to root this out before it could take hold. The poor psychoanalyst was bewildered. He could not figure out who was steering the ship and eventually threw up his hands and said that we seemed rather equally matched.

An example of this playful one-up-*personship* might be found in the fun we had with words, all kinds of words that ranged far and wide. I don't want to overstate this because his knowledge of languages and the etymology of words was astonishing, but if we played in the right field, we could have a great time. One night we were watching the televised coverage of the ceremony commemorating the anniversary of the Statue of Liberty. Ronald Reagan was going on about how we open our arms to those who come to our shores, while Nancy stood by in her smart red suit. Well, Bob and I started listing all the derogatory names that had been assigned to folks of various ethnicities who have come to this country, or who were waiting for us when we got here. We went on like that long after the ceremony was over and the TV was off. The words are nearly endless, and we hardly could have gotten them all. We were cueing off of each other, one word triggering another. We laughed till we were holding our sides and then laughed some more. What hypocrites we Americans can be—hypocrisy and noble aspiration, two sides of the same coin, our collective persona and shadow.

After Bob left the seminary and we moved to Florida, the rocking chair blessed Bob's new office, though the bottle of whisky with the red French tickler as its cork was no longer on the windowsill. Bob was now the executive director of a mental health center and often treating people in terrible trouble. He dressed in a necktie and wore a jacket. Jeans and his scandalous vocabulary came out only after hours. When I stopped by his office, I would make a point of sitting in the rocker. Then when we came to Little Rock, there just was not room for everything. We already had a house full of furniture, and to that we were adding the contents of two offices. Eventually some of the furniture would go to my downtown office, but in the meantime, things went into the attic. Unlike me, Bob had never found the rocker comfortable; the seat was too low to the floor for his long legs. So the chair was among things consigned to the attic to stay. Something more comfortable took its place in his library. When I would have reason to go up to the attic and see the rocker, it looked so forlorn growing more and more dusty in the shadows. But in the hours after Bob's death when the hospital bed was removed from the library, where for years he had lain amongst his beloved books, the hollow of that space echoed the hollowness of my heart and body; it cried out for something to come fill it. I sent a friend to the attic, and he brought the rocker down. Across the back of the chair would be hung the prayer shawl given to me by the All Saints Guild following Bob's funeral. Now this is the place where I sit every morning and evening to read the daily offices, holding the red leather-bound Prayer Book / Hymnal that Bob used at the altar for so many years.* Its large print suits my eyes. But the teapot? It sits on a shelf in the kitchen just a bit too high for my grasp. There is no longer that long, strapping bull of a man to reach it down and brew a cup of tea for me. Oh, Bobby, what lovely days have been ours!

* The formal name for the Prayer Book is The Book of Common Prayer. With the permission of the publishers, I will often refer to it as the Prayer Book and denote it with the initials BCP.

CHAPTER 3

The Crayolas and The Coloring Book

Tiger, tiger burning bright
In the forests of the night
What immortal hand or eye
Could frame thy fearful symmetry?

—William Blake, "The Tiger"

I was not the only person who found Bob to be a web of personalities. O. C. Edwards, a longtime colleague and friend, was aware of this multiplicity of characters. He describes this in a clever letter that was to be read at a roast of Bob that occurred on January 19, 1996, while Bob and I were in Florida and celebrating, with the congregation of Ascension, the thirty-fifth anniversary of Bob's ordination to the priesthood. O. C. writes:

> How long ago has it been that we have been a part of one another's lives? I think it was at Sewanee in 1961 ... The odd thing is that my impression of you then was of one quiet and well-behaved. No big cigar ... no stretching of the one syllable of the word for excrement into seven. No one could have guessed that you had ever been near

> a barnyard. At this time there was little sense of your promise, any glimmer, for instance that you would do the groundbreaking research on the holy canine, St. Bruno. No hint that you would commit poetry, that you would become a gadfly, prophet, and Kierkegaardian knight.[4]

(I promise my reader that I will come back to St. Bruno later. Don't scurry to look up that reference. It would be of no help here. This pertains to monkey business, nothing more.) O. C. encountered these various Bob Coopers just as I had—one well-behaved and courtly, another a completely uninhibited and feral snake charmer as well as the academician—at least these. This was the experience of many, and if one was not paying close attention, there might have been the impression that Bob was not in control of which facet of himself was allowed to display itself— but he was, at least the sweeping majority of the time.

That students continued to follow him long after their graduations was an indication of how important he was to us and what a powerful force he was in our formation. The mail from former students, those who were "on to" him, would arrive addressed to The Rev. Robert Swamp Cooper (his middle name was Marsh), or The Sometimes Rev. or The Irreverent or The Would-Be-If He-Could-Be Rev. Dr. Cooper. That latter was the concoction of a fellow student of mine and who, according to his account, enjoyed times in Bob's office when they shared "the sacrament of a smoke." (Taken from a letter read at the roast on January 19, 1996.) Perhaps the best of show was for The ir'Rev. Robert M. Cooper, A.B., M.Div., M.A., S.T.B., D.Div. INFJ, A&P, XXX; it was Bill Pregnall who wrote that one for the same occasion.[5] At one time, Bob and I lived on a street named Crested Butte. O. C. addressed a letter referring to the street as "Crested Butte [sic]." What wonderfully brilliant and funny friends Bob drew about himself. He relished these "disrespectful" jabs and greeted them with great delight and laughter. If I just close my eyes and let the years roll backward over me, I can almost see Bob coming in from the mailbox, with that long, slow lope, heading toward his library, and then hear him roaring with laughter as he read. Letters from his childhood friend Herbert Wentz probably took the prize for evoking the most laughter, but there were many others who came in a close second. Herb is dead now, and with the two there together, the heavens will never be the same.

O. C. and Jane have been dear friends, faithful friends to the end and beyond. They came to see us in the last months of Bob's life, and while they must have been as sad as I to see him fading away, they accepted him in this latter manifestation of his personality as they had accepted the others that had preceded it. I recall the way they said goodbye. They explained that they were finding the trip from Ashville to be a very hard one for them to continue making, and they doubted they would be back again. I think that Bob had exhausted himself in the visit, and I am not sure he understood what was being said, but we three did. What a sad moment. I did not realize then how close the end was, but I am thinking that they may have. God bless them; it takes courage to face another's undoing without flinching. They, as well as Ellen and Richard Price, who had known Bob since his first assignment as a young priest, were hovering presences through Bob's illness and since. I am grateful for them all. At one point early on, Richard remarked to me that Ellen found me to be courageous. Often I thought of that compliment, especially when I was flagging, and it helped me soldier on. It brought out the best in me when nothing else might have. What Ellen thought meant a great deal to me because she is an example of what a remarkable and courageous woman is.

Now, I promised I would tell you about St. Bruno. Bob said that the church had bred all the instinct out of Jesus; as a corrective, Bob decided that Jesus needed to have a dog that could carry that quality for "Our Most Blessed Lord." Now don't just read that last phrase in your ordinary internal reading voice. Instead you must draw your lips up tight in a little O and find your best pseudo-English accent like so many of the prissy clergy that Bob had not suffered gladly in his time in the church. Now read it again, and you get a hint of Bob when he mimicked these fellows. The following poem written in the spring of 1984 will give you a glimpse into Bob's disdain of all this ecclesiastical tomfoolery.

The Immanent John Leadmine

"The immanent John Leadmine will be our guest
preacher this week," and if we get there early

enough just imagine we might see him
when he shifts to transcendent as he surely will
during his time *with us* and the choir will sing
O they will want to sing so sing out
"O to be God now that Easter and he are here!"

If anybody phones me tell 'em I'm meditating.
(Cooper)[6]

So, to work against this nonsense that can break out in the church, the dog was born, or perhaps not exactly born, since the creed Bob had fashioned stated quite clearly that the beast was Very dog of Very Dog. Bob had named the dog Bruno, and somewhere along the way, the animal was canonized, henceforth to be referred to as St. Bruno. (Now, to prevent confusion, there are various saints with the name Bruno, but this dog is definitely not among them!)

Well, you can imagine how this newborn legend of a sainted dog took on a life of its own. There were many aspirants who wished to become members of the Holy Order of St. Bruno, and Bob, being in charge of such matters, turned no one away. Over the years, we were overrun with dog paraphernalia that people sent in honor of the critter. One that was particularly hideous arrived on the scene before I did. It was a very large painting, the canvas of which had been used and reused so many times that the layers of paint were many and cracking. *Pentimento* would be too elegant a word for its condition; it was simply a wreck. The colors were so dark that it was pretty much impossible to see what the subject matter was. That horrible thing made it from its origins to Texas to Dunedin, Florida, and on to Little Rock. It is in the attic now, but it will never be seen again because, as dark as it is, it will lurk unseen in the shadows of the eves to the end of time. I do from time to time think I hear it panting, or perhaps that is chanting. It is hard to tell the difference with a dog.

On one occasion, I was sitting not far from Bob when we had some uppity ecclesiastical dignitary come to speak *at* us in the seminary chapel. The man had mounted the pulpit and from it was inflicting upon us one platitude strung against another. Heretics are far more preferable to humdrummers who bore holes in your head until your brains drain out. I was sitting not far from Bob, so I got some sense of his restlessness. First he began to fidget in his seat, crossing right foot over left knee, followed by a shift to the left. Bob reached his limit long before the preacher reached his. Finally it happened. With a not so *sotto voce,* we all heard a clear "Horseshit!" coming from Bob's direction. Well, there you have it. That was one facet of Bob, and perhaps the one most often spoken of, but there were others, and I am so sorry when those get overlooked.

For the same roast I mentioned above, Bruce McMillan had written some funny memories, but then he stopped to say these words:

> Bob also taught us more than just ethics and moral theology. He taught us how to be good pastors and priests. He was a pastor to us and we learned from watching him how "mercy and truth are met together," and that righteousness and peace really do have to kiss each other in the pastoral relationship. As a priest, he was ... a vision of unrivaled piety and presence at the altar. If you want to know what an icon of Christ is, Bob is a quick study in that.[7]

I can testify to that as well. Before a service, or a sermon, or a speaking engagement, Bob would move into some curious space, as if he were passing over into the ancient shaman's *temanos* that is real but unknowable to the human eye—into a holy space, that place where the vague outlines of the interior life of the Almighty can be glimpsed. He sat in "the gateless gate," even if for just a time. And more than that, Bob could bring what he experienced back to those who then listened to him speak. In short, Bob was inspired by his intimate relationship with God. I learned to anticipate these times of withdrawal and give him all the room he needed as he made this interior journey. To a certain extent, I knew it because I had experienced it in myself when some solemn task lay ahead of me. But while I might have experienced it from the inside, I had never watched the transformation in someone from the outside until the first time I saw Bob dig deep into the unseen world of the Divine and then bring back its treasures. The Greeks would have called him a *psychopomp* guiding the soul between the worlds of the human and Divine. And if all of this sounds too grand or spiritual, remember that it was balanced by an outlandishness that was as earthy as the other was ethereal.

Letter after letter from former students tell of how Bob took them in and helped them through difficult and sad places in their lives. A former classmate of mine who is no longer living but who is remembered lovingly by me, Lyman Reed (or "*Lyperson*" as Bob called him), wrote once to Bob of his amusement that there had been those who were actually intimidated by Bob. Lyman knew how to make the distinction between Bob the approachable, even playful, and the intellect of Bob that could knock you back on your heels if you did not know to anticipate it.

While some were served tea, others were offered cigars; we were all given a safe place to unburden our souls. And yet, despite all of this, Bob was a lonely man. With interests so deep and varied, few could match his intellect, and wherever he went, the insecure were envious of him. He was also competitive, and if you wanted to be small and argumentative, he could beat you at your own game before you knew what was happening. Bob had also made enemies because of his involvement in controversial issues such as the civil rights movement, the opposition to the war in Vietnam, his efforts to promote the regularization of the ordination of women, and later, though slower in coming to it, the struggle for gay rights. He took on the entrenched powers that be, and he bore the scars. He truly sought to make a difference to the ills of the world and twice left positions that he held under a cloud because he was moving contrary to the leadership of the schools where he served. I am sure that he had regrets—one cannot be as introspective or empathetic as he was and not have regrets—but he never regretted the hell he had raised on these campuses, even though he was hurt deeply by the rejection.

After Bob's one-word critique of that sermon in our dignitary-visited chapel, I went out and bought a big ol', thick coloring book and some jumbo Crayolas. The next day in chapel, I sat down beside Bob and, just before the service started, gave him the book and crayons. I suggested that they would be helpful in keeping him well behaved during the service. How he loved it! Those who did not know him well were not sure how I had gotten out alive because they were certain he would find it an offense. Like the painting of Bruno, that coloring book followed us from Texas to Florida and back to Little Rock; it was among Bob's treasures. Bob took these jokes well because he knew he could be an arrogant SOB, and he knew he deserved being taken down from time to time. That was one of his frequent observations. "I deserved it!" he would say. He was a target drawn in broad strokes and therefore not hard to miss. His friends were good at hitting the bull's-eye. So were his enemies.

One very difficult and restless afternoon when Bob could no longer concentrate well enough to read and did not want to watch any more stories on his DVD player, I was feeling desperate for some way to keep him entertained. He did not want to make cookies or go outside. (He became afraid of going out.) It was one of those desperate times when he, like many dementia patients, wanted his life to end. He was begging me to tell him how to do it. I needed to find a diversion fast, when suddenly I remembered the coloring book. It was on a high shelf in the closet off my study. I had kept it there with toys and board games for the grandchildren, but for some reason, I had never pulled it down for them. They were all grown up now and had no need for any of the toys stored there. But now I did. I climbed up and got them from the shelf. I gave the book to Bob along with his jumbo Crayolas and watched as he contentedly spent the afternoon trying to stay in the lines and showing me proudly each page as he had colored away. He never finished that book, and with a certain amount of anguish, I threw it away after his death, along with the thousands of pages of manuscripts and letters. How quickly it all drifts away. It would have seemed that, like Macbeth, we had now found that all was little but "the sere, the yellow leaf" to those looking on from the outside. But to those who loved him so, to Bruce and me who had to see his papers to their end, these bits and pieces were as sacred as the life that created them. It hurt so deeply to see them go. At the end of a day of hard work, Bruce and I would be covered in dust like children at play. "Dust thou art, and unto dust shalt thou return" (Gen 3:19 King James Version). Some of the papers and publications are still stored in banker's boxes and his file cabinets. I could stand just so much destruction. I will come back to it in time—perhaps. But not now, not just now. Now I will read it and touch it and thank the Almighty for the creator of it.

Even still, it can sweep over me like a bad dream; and then, in the next moment, I have a sense of his presence as strong and as alive as ever. And I have this growing confidence that nothing, absolutely nothing is lost, that our gifts and talents and passions find their source in the Divine and therefore return to the Divine. We, and all that we have been, are headed home. And love? Love most of all is inviolate.

The first Christmas after Bob's passing, I was borne up by the presence of a dear little six-year-old who is my great-granddaughter. I found myself shopping again for a coloring book and Crayolas. Bob loved children and would have delighted in Jayden's presence that Christmas. And how excited Bob would have been at the birth of great-grandbaby, Aria, who was born almost to the day of the first anniversary of his passing. I find myself thinking, *If only he could have been here for this,* and then I realize that he is; it is only I who is lost in the illusion of time and space. He is not. As Yeats put it, his face is merely hidden "amid a crowd of stars."

CHAPTER 4

The Dancer

I cannot dance upon my Toes—
No Man instructed me—
But oftentimes, among my mind
A Glee possesseth me.

—Emily Dickinson, "I Cannot Dance Upon my Toes"

Bob had said to me, sitting there in his office, that he had always wanted to learn to dance, that the motion of the human body was the most beautiful of the arts and he would like to be a part of that. We agreed then and there that if the opportunity ever came, we would take dance lessons. That did not mean that we would ever be able to do it together, but it did mean that at some point, before it was too late, we would learn to dance. It was a deal that we made with ourselves in the other's company.

As a child, I had been given lessons in ballet, tap, and ballroom. I had never resented being expected to attend these dance classes because I had enjoyed them all—unlike the eight years of piano that we'd all suffered through. When dancing, I felt graceful; whether I was or not I do not know, but I felt that way, and I always looked forward to doing that again. I look back on those times with great pleasure. Early on, I had tapped away in a Carmen Miranda costume, fruit atop my head and all—Carmen, the original food truck. I had been a cloud in a ballet number in which my scarves had been used in the end to cover the sun. As an adult, I had taken tap again to drive away the sorrow after the loss of children in a botched adoption. The dance number we learned had been choreographed for the music composed by Marvin Hamlish for *A Chorus Line*. The lyrics, though not a part of what we were doing at the time, were about having suffered loss but having done it all for love. That seems to be a theme that has reappeared from time to time in my life, and the music was perfect for that period.

One Christmas, friends of mine, Lynn and Russell, threw a party in his condo, which was decorated impeccably and was high above the city with a fine view of the lights below. Earlier that day, I had been in Bob's office when he got some phone call; I truly cannot recall about what. Bob would say later that evening as we stood on the balcony looking out over the city that he hoped he had not "compromised" me by having taken that call. I said to him something that he would repeat time and again when showing me off to his friends. "She tells me that she has a perfect memory; she can forget everything." Then he would wait for laughter to follow. It is just about true. I forget names, numbers, sometimes even faces, but what I recall with extreme accuracy are the things that matter to me. I remember people's stories and what people have to say to one another, the mood that was felt at a particular place or time—the things that carry with them some sort of power within the psyche. The Swiss psychiatrist Carl Jung made a similar observation of himself; he recalled the things that carried meaning. For all else, Bob came to serve as my memory. I relied on him for so much, so, in a real sense, if he was losing his memory, I was losing mine as well. I still catch myself thinking that I will ask him, only to realize that I cannot.

One of those things that mattered to me though, enough to remember, was what Bob said about the art of dance. Walking into the party that evening, I had seen, lining the walls of the lobby and hallways, various bronze sculptures by a San Antonio artist named Villareal. The particular one that caught my eye was a seated ballerina, her back pulled against some stiffness, seated with the soles of her feet together and her hands grasping her toes. The next time Bob and I were in his office, he asked if I had seen this particular ballerina, the same one that caught my eye. I made up my mind that somehow I was going to get her, and I did. She is beautiful. It was close to my time to leave seminary before the sculptor and I struck a deal that I could manage. I had bought it to mark my graduation and to put it in my home in Houston—the one I never occupied.

My supposed departure and Bob's fiftieth birthday were looming; he was sliding into a dark depression. Everything seemed to be tearing at him. I thought that if perhaps I gave him my dancer, it would help to pull him through this bad patch, but he told me that I would have to take care of the dancer for him, thereby refusing to accept her. There was something ominous about the way he said it that gave me a glimpse into just how deep his depression was. I was not the only person who had seen this; there were others. I would learn later that by the end of that summer, Will had confronted Bob about it and seen him into the care of a psychiatrist. Later when the work of therapy came to a hiatus, Bob told me that that he (Bob) had become a hero to himself. He had fought hard for his life. Nothing like this would happen again until the depression of dementia began to break through from time to time, and then only periodically when my task was not to be the dark cloud that covers the sun but just the reverse.

As time unwound itself and gave Bob a new life, the dancer's home came to be his home as well. I see her every day, and when I do, I think of him running his hand down the curve of her back when she was within his reach. He loved touching; he loved being touched. I am so grateful that the ballerina ultimately became a source of joy to him as well as to me. Now I once again take care of her for him. We are blessed with many lovely things, but Bob had his favorites, and this piece was among them.

I can't think of him touching the ballerina without also thinking of Bob and our visit to the studio of the sculptor Allan Houser. He was an "Indian," as Mr. Houser would have put it. I can no longer recall how we came by the invitation, but it was accepted, and we were taken about the studio by Houser himself. He also walked us down the hill to show us a kiva that he was so proud of. It was carved out of the dusty, dry hillside and was used for tribal gatherings. His sculptures were scattered throughout the grove of pinyon trees. Bob was taken with the man and his work. The pieces were massive, and the studio reflected that by the presence of cables and pulleys and a loading area large enough for trucks to back up to it. I do believe Bob was ready to move everything we had out onto the street if he could have brought a sculpture home to our condo, but he had to settle for a maquette of a larger piece called *Sun Catcher*, which we had come across in a gallery earlier that day.

The Sun Catcher is a craggy, old woman with a hawkish nose. She is dressed in long robes that cover her body. Her hidden feet are sole to sole, and her knees are out to the side much like the ballerina. This pose forms of her robes a basin in her lap. We always kept her in the sunlight, and, almost without fail, Bob would dip his fingers in the pool of light and make the sign of the cross as though he were dipping his fingers in holy water as he entered a church; this was the poetry of Bob's life, not just what was written, read, and recited. I don't recall that I ever did that myself so long as Bob was living, but now I do it as if somehow it is a ritual that must be maintained. I find it curious how we gather up around ourselves the habits of those we have loved as a way of honoring them, of keeping them around us—or at least I have.

One Thanksgiving, dear friends, recently married, "called in their strays," as they put it. They recalled vividly what holidays could be for single people. Invitees were each to bring that dish without which Thanksgiving was not Thanksgiving. I chose the turkey and dressing. For our hostess, it was cans of LeSuere peas, to which we all had a great laugh—not because it was strange but because it was familiar. I can't remember what others brought, but we had a great meal. It was a lovely evening, and I remember it partly because it was the first time that I would meet Bruce—he who would be such a great friend over the next thirty years, even to the extent of placing himself on the emotional altar of helping me sort out Bob's things when the music had finally stopped.

Bob had been asked to pick me up that evening; I would have had a real struggle getting myself and the turkey and dressing and messy gravy to the party without spilling something on the car floor. We arrived late, and as I carried the dressing and gravy, Bob got the turkey and shut the car door. As I stepped onto the front porch, the door flew open, and all asked like one, "Where is the turkey?" Not a hello in the bunch. In a somewhat sardonic tone, I replied, "Oh, they're both behind me." Bob missed what I said, but he heard the laughter; someone had to tell him that once again he had been the butt of the joke. But that was just fine with him; he laughed louder than all. He simply loved being paid attention to. And he had a taste for smart-ass women.

There were only six of us, but we had enough fun for sixty—eating, drinking good wine, savoring the company of bright and interesting people. Then somebody put the music on, and eventually there came up the Eurythmics singing "Missionary Man." Bob listened to the words, then wanted it played again. Dressed in a gray three-piece suit with his Western hat on his big head and clamping a huge cigar between his teeth, Fr. Cooper began gyrating about the room like nothing I had ever seen. His motions resembled more nearly those of a deranged monkey than any other of God's creatures. It was the funniest thing. I howled with laughter; we all did. As tears of glee had their way with my mascara, Bob stopped as suddenly as he had started and looked at me intently. "You are not afraid of me," he said. I know I must have looked puzzled. Why on earth should I be afraid? Then as suddenly as he had stopped, he resumed wildly moving about the room.

Later, on the way home, I asked him why there might have been any issue about my being afraid of him. He just said simply that there were those whom he frightened when he got crazy like that. I never pressed remarks of that sort. Later, when I found his journals, I saw that he returned to this theme of others being afraid of him. Some had said so, and others he guessed were. Perhaps in the case of colleagues, this can be explained—not excused but explained. Bob moved against the flow, and this set the trustees against the faculty. Nobody wanted to kick up the dust, and Bob was a dust-kicker-upper if ever there were one. Nevertheless, how sad. Fear and love are mutually exclusive; no wonder that, from our first conversation, Bob seemed to be such a lonely person. He later told me of this, but once again, the pain seemed muted by the passing of years. The slow, quiet conversation had betrayed his passion. But in the journals, the emotion is raw and painful in its writing.

Years before that delightful Thanksgiving evening, Bob had published a group of poems in the "Ratherview." There was one that I simply couldn't find my way into. The images it created were lovely, but I wanted to anchor it in meaning of some sort. One day after chapel, I asked him if I could make an appointment to talk about the poem. It was a week or so before we could discuss it, but when we did, I admitted my obtuseness. A few words from him, and the poem fell open for me. He didn't explain it; he just told me what he was feeling and thinking when he wrote it. Just as I was leaving his office, he told me that I should not be embarrassed about asking him to talk about the meaning behind the poem, because he wanted to be understood, he wanted to explain. He said he wanted to be known, but not all were interested in knowing him. He made no further comment at that time, and I had the good sense to know that no comment of mine was expected, nor would it have been appropriate. I just stood there holding the doorknob in silence as a certain grief worked its way through the room. I could not be for him all that he needed in that moment, but before I left, I told him I was glad he was my friend. Perhaps I could be accused of having changed the subject and abandoning him to the bleakness. On the other hand, perhaps I had done just the opposite. When reading his journals, I found that he went to some pains to explain an episode of not being known and the pain it caused him. Again I say, Bob was a lonely man; all he ever wanted from any of us was to be known.

What helped me come to know him to the extent that I could was that Bob and I are much alike, and also because we had begun as adult friends. I had the opportunity to learn that he could live with a certain level of not being known, so long as he was paid attention to in his idiosyncrasies and assured of love. He also did not mind being engaged and questioned, even challenged, so long as those two pieces were in place—attentiveness and love. That is not so different from most of us. I had known Bob thirty-five years at the time of his death, and I had discovered something new about him each day, and particularly during his illness when the persona began to give way and the shadow began to appear with more clarity. In some ways, he was at his most interesting during that time.

After his death, I found two banker's boxes filled with poems, most of which were never published or even submitted for publication; they cut too close to the bone. Some of the most beautiful of them had never seen the light of day, I am quite sure. There was something in him that did not want to be completely known. I know that desire for a private place within myself; perhaps it is in all of us. I do not know. But I think that is why I did not always rush to probe into his interior life. Even so, Bob told me a great deal without my questioning. In a love relationship, it is so much better to hear one's beloved speak as freely and as slowly as he likes, rather than to interrogate; or at least that seemed right to me. Bob was a gift, and I value him; he was not mine to change or cure. He was given to me to love and cherish, nothing more. Eventually his inner world made its way to me but never in its entirety. I can say this: Bob was a feeling in search of a reason, and it was that quest for self-understanding that drove his desire to read and learn as much as he could—history, philosophy, theology, the arts, science, psychology, and more still.

But dance, I was talking about dance, not poetry or human complexities. When the time came that Bob and I could take those dance lessons, we did, and we did them together. Bob could sing well but not dance. Oh, what a struggle he had. I could never understand it; if you can keep time well enough to sing, why can't you keep time well enough to dance? Bob was not a graceless man; quite the contrary. But only with real effort did we begin to learn the Texas two-step, the fox-trot, and the most fun (and difficult) of all, the tango. We were doing it. Oh, glee! About this time, one of our friends and her friend became serious dancers, and the tango was their favorite. They had been dancing together for a long time compared to us. For some special occasion, they rented a dance hall. For the first time, Bob and I stepped onto the dance floor with someone other than our instructor looking on. We were doing quite well, given that we were beginners at dancing together. Then came the tango. We started quite nicely, and then about midway through, Bob came down with one of his "spells." He started pulling me about the floor like a madman. I was in tow so could not get a good view of what was happening, but I rather think that Bob was channeling Groucho Marx, tearing about the dance floor with knees bent. Once he had come to himself, I asked him what on earth had just happened. He named one of our friends and his wife who had been just sitting there all evening, glumly looking on dance after dance, the tension between them growing. Bob said something to the effect that our friend was a good guy and that he (Bob) would rather have the man's friendship than be a "fancy dancer." So, except for the nights that we slow danced in the kitchen, we just danced like monkeys. It's a lot more fun. But then, dancing in the kitchen is fun too.

As I have said, I was attracted to Bob because he was an intellectual and profound thinker. I admired him as a writer about important things and a wordsmith who communicated from the soul. He was a warrior for justice and the good and the beautiful. He was a devout man and confessed sinner who strove to honor the Divine. I was made breathless by him because he was an exquisite poet and lover. I admired him when he was courageous in the face of his own undoing. But just as importantly, he was lovable because he was funny, a comic, the joker, the whirling dervish, a shape-shifter, and wild man—and still more. But I take comfort in the belief that he knew, should I have learned even more of him than I already knew, I would love that too.

As I write this, I think of Elie Wiesel's description of the Hasidim dancing in the cattle cars as they rolled toward Birkenau because it was the time appropriate to usher in Simchat Torah. They would not be deterred from their call. Their misfortune can be seen as a symptom indicative of their call, a call to steadfastness, a call to wholeness. This is the same irrepressible response to a calling that Habakkuk evidences following the devastation of Judah.

> Although the fig tree shall not blossom, neither shall fruit be in the vines; the labor of the olive shall fail, and the fields shall yield no meat; the flock shall be cut off from the fold, and there shall be no herd in the stalls: Yet I will rejoice in the Lord, I will joy in the God of my salvation. (Hab. 3:17–18, King James Version)

Habakkuk is not so much living the call as the call is living Habakkuk, and I believe that to be true of Bob as well. That was never more apparent than during and after the diagnosis of his illness, as day after day he surrendered more and more of himself, to what he could not know. He waited in faith for the end to come. Yes there were times of terror and fear when he wanted it to end. But for the most part, he danced his way to Birkenau.

I long for the day when I will dance again with the monkey dancer.

Plié, relevé, tendu, and close.

CHAPTER 5

The Flint, The Preacher, and The Fool

In a theater, it happened that a fire started off stage. The clown came out to tell the audience. They thought it was a joke and applauded. He told them again, and they became still more hilarious. This is the way ... that the world will be destroyed—amid the universal hilarity of wits and wags who think it is all a joke.

—Søren Kierkegaard, *Either/Or*, Vol. 1 of 2[8]

Bob often said that had he been aspiring to ordination at the time that I had, he would have never made the cut. That is likely right, and it is sad. With the exception of more than a few truly extraordinary people, the blood has gone out of those receiving the nod—from my limited point of view, that is. And at the same time, the church takes a risk when it ordains a Bob Cooper. He was in many respects well outside the norm, not easily bridled, and certainly unpredictable. The church needed his mind, and so it put up with much, at least the majority of the time.

In the mid-sixties, the bottom seemed to fall out for Bob. He was a college chaplain, teaching at the university, and working on two masters in two different schools. He was very nearly swamped by stress and a sense of lack; he felt as if he were coming undone. He had been unwise in that he was not seeking help and had waited an unnecessarily long time before getting it. As a consequence, he had put everything at risk because he was too prideful to seek help sooner. It was not until he had let himself fall in love that he came to his senses. Nothing came of this, but he frightened himself enough that he sought help. He told Terry Holmes, who was his dear friend and supervisor, and together they told their kind and understanding bishop about Bob's fragile and vulnerable state. Terry and the bishop had gotten him to a psychiatrist, a Dr. Olivier, a Freudian psychoanalyst, who helped Bob find ways to channel his memories of childhood and his fragile emotional state into a powerfully introspective, poetic force that Bob would draw on for decades to come. It was as if, with the doctor's help, Bob was able to find in this a muse from which he would draw creative energy in his teaching, preaching, and writing of poetry. He was eventually drawn back to himself with a new strength and clarity of values, his gifts enhanced. It was sometime after this that the prolific writing of poetry and the journals began.

Childhood's Nocturnal Journey

By telling me one day your maiden name
You divulged to me the dark secrets
Of the grand mysteries of ancient Greeks,

Through your name, I seek and fail at the same

Time to have you. Turning it over now
In my mind, and on my tongue, your lover,
I know and have you as did no other.
Yet your body, always the lively vow

Of your presence escapes me like a wild
Thing. Not to have your body but only
Your plain name is to leave yourself lonely
And apart. It is to see a dark child,

Not born of our union, pass in the dead

Of night my bedroom door, and quietly flee
From me down childhood's nocturnal journey.
It is to turn in my large, lonely bed.
(Cooper)[9]

The force of this experience and the gratitude for his escape from its madness were present in his poems and his sermons throughout his life. The influence of that muse was certainly not dispelled by my presence; I simply had to travel along with her. Hers was the potency of the road not taken, and its melancholy tone continued to be with him. When reading his poems, I know when it is her power that speaks, and I bow to her. From this time, Bob learned what it was to be, as he put it, re-membered, put back together like the dry bones in the desert, and when he spoke of this re-membering, it was something of which he had direct knowledge. I never knew Bob to blame anyone for this episode in his life other than his own sick soul. He would draw on this experience time and again in classes he taught as well as sermons and talks he gave. I remember sitting in class and being astounded at how vulnerable he would make himself. I feared that he could be hurt again, that these revelations could be used against him. If he had this concern, he never expressed it at the time. He simply spoke of "having to get his head fixed" and how he was nearly out of his mind with the sorrow in his life. I doubt that he had a student on that campus who did not know who Dr. Olivier was, and who was not given the opportunity to discover that the day might come when they would need a Dr. Olivier of their own.

I have listened to recordings of a weekend series of talks Bob gave in the Diocese of Iowa in the late seventies. Once again, he goes back to his time with a psychiatrist. In these lectures, he was talking about ministry and the importance of being the fool when that is what is called for. Admitting to his frailties before this gathering of strangers was to be a fool; speaking publicly before strangers in this way was to risk his life in the church like a jester making foolish the medieval king and his court. In both instances, his listeners and the king could have exercised an authority over the fool. Bob could have destroyed his reputation taking these risks, but he must have considered that more than that was at stake. Someone in the audience asked if it was not dangerous to be a fool, and he simply responded, "Yes." This same person then countered that it made her afraid. To this, Bob responded, "Me too. You can be misunderstood." Clearly he knew what he was doing and what was laid open and left unprotected—vulnerable. He was not a buffoon, but he was like a clown—sad because he saw what the world was and called it out, and joyful because he knew what the world could be. He truly believed power can only be conquered by weakness.

One day in his office, he told me more of the near catastrophe of the sixties. There was a sadness in the telling of it, a sadness for the harm he had done to himself and those who loved him, but because he told of it in some detail, there was also a clear knowledge that he had grown to the depth that he was able to find because of the acknowledgment of it all. He neither advertised it nor hid it; the telling or not telling was based on my need to hear and not on Bob's need to talk. He had found peace in it long before. He was admired by most of my classmates for the courage of owning his own humanity, and it was out of this that a powerful ministry to the troubled grew and took hold. When he told me of it, it was clear that he considered this self-neglect to be one of the worst, if not the worst, things he had ever experienced. The regret of pridefulness was there, but so was the self-forgiveness. It had been a terrible time for all involved, but he had emerged from it with a clearer sense of himself and his limits, as well as with a more intimate relationship with the Holy One. He had been brought low and humbled, but he had also begun the learning of letting go, being himself, owning his darker side, and becoming genuine. This is a process that I suppose never has an end, but the undertaking of it is true piety. This was most likely the single most important thing in Bob's life. Without it, he could not have been half the priest, pastor, teacher, therapist, poet, human being that he became. Nothing slips through the fingers of the Divine. Good can be made from anything; it only awaits our realization of who is the potter and who is the clay.

He knew what a terrible prig I was and that I had been put in the place of having to prove that I could be suitable of ordination, which only made my prudishness all the more inflamed. By being told his story, he was offering me an opportunity to either be horrified by his human frailty and run from it, or to grow up in the knowledge that we all have failings, even those whom we admire the most. My idol exposed his own clay feet, and that fairly early on. It was his example that helped me learn to take ownership of my own shadowy heart and come to grips with it. The result was one of considerable release from the drive to be the perfect seminarian, at least in his company. His teaching and presence among those who were being trained for the priesthood would have been worthless if he had hidden from us the truth of who he was and the truths of his own life. There were people on that campus, people I loved, who did hide, and it was as if the phony piety was more of a flashing light over the problems than a cover of them. In Bob's case, he knew himself fairly well, and from that he offered solace to others.

One lovely story that Bob referred to often was an experience that had occurred on one Ash Wednesday. A mother, holding her small child on her shoulder, came to the altar rail for the imposition of ashes. He rubbed an ash cross on the mother's brow as the baby continued to look away. Bob reached around the baby's little head and placed ashes on his forehead. Bob wrote in a note to me, a note that he knew he would beat home, "I don't recall ever having put ashes on the head of an infant before."* With smudge on forehead, the little guy whipped his head around, and Bob was looking into these wide-open baby eyes as Bob said, "Remember you are dust, and to dust you shall return" (BCP, p.265). Yes, even this little innocent with his gorgeous brown eyes was like all the rest of us, the spirit of the Divine invested in the frailty of human flesh that will fall short—so short. Bob knew this; we are children of the Holy One and children of dust. Dust will out, and so will grace, if we choose to have any of it.

On the day of my graduation from seminary, I learned of a true horror in my own life. There was not another person on that campus to whom I would have turned for solace or direction other than Bob. When I told him of it, he quoted the line from Tennessee Williams' *The Night of the Iguana*. At least he began it, "Nothing human disgusts me ..." We finished it together. For the next half hour or so, we sat, knees almost touching, as I wept and he prayed. All my hopes and expectations were being dashed. I would drive to Houston the next day and tell my mentor and then my

* Bob wrote notes to me when he was away. Sometimes these were written at the beginning of his trip and mailed, or at other times on his flight home, but there was always a note for each day—that or a poem. Other notes were left on the kitchen counter when I was away when he left home. I loved reading them then, and I love them now even more. We rarely ever dated these notes; I suppose we thought we would go on forever and never would have the desire to reconstruct the past.

bishop what was happening. When the Bishop heard what I had to say, I was dismissed. That was a Saturday.

Bob was out of town that weekend, but early Monday I called and asked if I could come by his office. As I tried to tell him about my visit with the bishop and its consequences, our conversation was interrupted five times by clergy who had some relationship to me that gave them some pastoral responsibility for my well-being. All washed their hands of me and told Bob that they knew he would look after me. The self-professed fallen one was the one who was expected to stand tall. But that is enough of that for now. I will return to it later.

Bob was a far better preacher than most and was generally orthodox in his preaching, but he was also a spellbinding sidewinder of a preacher. He was the academic one second, and then in the next, he was revealing the spirituality of one who was deeply steeped in the mystics and given to a serious and ongoing mapping of the topography of his own soul. Bob truly sought for God despite his foibles, or perhaps because of them. He was Eastern and Western. He moved easily among the philosophies of the Greeks. He loved the writings of St. Augustine of Hippo and was comfortable with his knowledge and use of theologians from Aquinas, to Luther, to Calvin, to Barth. He knew the heresies and loved to tease his students and colleagues by deliberately dancing along the edges of them and saying so. So familiar was he with the various disciplines that he was forever winding them together in his sermons, layer upon layer so that they took on a sense of depth; they taught and inspired at whatever level one was able to hear.

There were regular characters that would populate his sermons—the backwoods preacher like those he was familiar with in North Carolina when he was growing up, the uppity pseudo-Englishman whose piety was unsurpassed, as well as a half-dozen others. It would always be the pseudo piety of the clergy that came in for the worst of it. A former student of his, Dale Coleman, wrote this note after Bob's passing: "What a wonderful, brilliant man and priest … he was amazing in his straightforward integrity, and always clever in attacking clergy pretensions. He was a joy to be around, and true about his faith in Jesus. On his end table would be found *Freud: Biologist of the Mind,* and a volume of Barth's *Church Dogmatics.*"[10] Yes, that is the Bob I knew, a whirl of things all going on at one time. He also loved poetry, and that would find its way in there too—his poetry and that of others.

One evening I overheard Will ask Bob what he was going to preach on the next day in chapel. Bob answered, "Oh some Gospel and some dramer." (That's southern for drama, something that Will, a fellow North Carolinian, would have known.) I was present for that sermon, but I don't remember the Gospel part—not at all. What I do remember was Bob stalking around the edges of the congregation, his boots pounding into the stone floor and his alb flowing behind. All the while, he was striking huge chunks of flint—sparks flying. God help us all, he looked like some prophet escaped from the pages of the Bible on the lectern. He was speaking the whole time, but that was lost on me. I just remember that he was on fire for God! And I was inspired by the power of that.

In Memoriam: Elmer Gantry

Word-intoxicated
Fool for Christ's sake
Halting, blathering
Cursing priestcraft,
Dresser of sycamores
Wild-eyed, locust-fed
Get your head on a platter
Got your head up a skirt
Ashes to ashes
Dirt to dirt
Eloi, eloi
Sawn asunder
Thorn in the flesh
Thrown to the lions
Flung in a pit
Hung on a tree
Cursed
Jeezsus!
(Cooper)[11]

When Bruce and I first sat down to the melancholy office of sorting through Bob's things, I thought we would find his sermons, and I looked forward to reading them. Bruce thought he had found a few, but even those disappeared in the disarray. To my dismay, what I found there were only notes Bob had made to himself, and they were written in Greek and sometimes Hebrew. What sermons exist are ones that someone has transcribed from tapes, and those are few. I have kept a few of the scribbles. My Greek is pathetic, and my Hebrew is very nearly gone altogether (assuming it was ever present). I've worked hours at translating some of these notes; his handwriting is atrocious. Mostly I just hold the pages and remember—just remember. I later found a few tapes that I have had preserved on disks. I listen to his voice as I fall asleep at night—so charmed and charming was he. How is it that such power can come down to just these bits of paper? I have to believe that something is stored up somewhere in the heart of the Almighty—that it found its source there and it has returned to that source, as has Bob.*

During those seminary years, as I listened to his sermons and in our conversations I sensed that he was telling more and more about himself in ways he had not done before. I feared for him. He had few secrets, but he spoke to us in such code that most never knew with certainty what personal stuff we had been given. There were glaring clues that things were shaky in his life, but I wanted to miss them, at least for a time, though I couldn't. In the last weeks of my senior year, my own life and hopes were shaky at best, and I needed a confidant who was absolutely safe. He knew that and was protective of me even though this pushed him even further into a lonely place. I saw what was happening, but I was too weak to make it different; consequently, I had no idea how much trouble he was in. And if I had, I would have been helpless to make a difference. When all of those calls came that day as I tried to tell him of my situation, he was very somber. He reminded me that he had taken on speaking obligations that would occupy him for the next month, but he would be home and able to see me on Mondays. He called Will as we sat there, and the two of them agreed on a psychiatrist whom I should see. Will would take over from there.

* Recently my granddaughter, Bailey, found, high on a shelf, a box of ninety-seven tapes that have been transferred to discs. I look forward to hearing all of them.

Bob was charmed by Japanese rock gardens and had created his version of one in his backyard. Along its boundary, he had built a stacked-stone wall. In that spring of my senior year, he told me, and I read it again recently in his journals, that a couple of stones had slipped from their places in the morning; he had set them back as they belonged. Then that evening, when sitting by the wall, it collapsed. This time the breach was great enough that it could not simply be repaired. He would have to begin again, and he did not have the energy or desire to do it.

This Is for John

This is for John because I think of you
a long way from here and know how
the September light will fall soon on you
in colors that you used to see
that fail now in the light that remains

We never know what remains of a life
This is so simple since the end surprises
in the predictions we knew how to make
in the wide ignorance of your when and mine

I am gathering stones today (I did yesterday)
against the coming closure I shape them
in patterns (A Zen gardener) a circle here
there the necessary triangle and the square
some water the pebbled sea the waves
I leave by design the space I hope to call
in the next breath but one freedom
and in the last yes
(Cooper)

Because Bob saw an enchantment in the world, he was stunned by the caving in of the wall and mused aloud about its being an omen; he wondered if he should attribute to it a greater meaning. I did not press him further. I knew what he was thinking; much was caving in for him. The year was ending, and another set of people to whom he had become attached would be leaving—I included, we thought.

If one believes in omens, as he had, this one was borne out. Much in his life would collapse, turn in on itself, and fall to bits that summer. In time, to his great surprise, he was able to build a new garden—to start from scratch and become fresh again. But the price was a high one. Before that could happen, he would have to admit to me that he was so undone by his own life that he was worthless to me. Through that summer, we talked on the phone occasionally and briefly. By fall, I had begun to get myself settled, with the enormous help of friends and a professional. That was when I got the call asking if I knew where Bob was. I had no idea. He was missing, and people were fearing suicide. In the end, it was just hysteria; he had driven to San Antonio to see his psychiatrist. All was well. I was shaken though. What would it be like to be in a world where Bob was not?

When eventually I heard from him, I did not turn him away, though he was not the Bob I had known. But he and his psychiatrist were doing good work. Mine was too stern and Freudian for my Jungian taste, but she had gotten me on my feet. In the end, both Bob and I survived but only with the help of other people. While we cared deeply for each other, we could only have done each to the other harm. It would be a while before we could be ourselves again—ourselves but very different too. In some major ways, we didn't even recognize ourselves. And we had grown so much stronger.

Aphrodite is here
Hermes has come into the room
Here then the translation begins
the blood into fire and light
Here dark Taurus burns in the mind's pyre
It is salt alone at last we taste
the blood the sea the stirred womb
the final fire and the salt on the threshold*

—Robert Cooper, "A House in the Zodiac"[12]

---

* Salt on the threshold is a means of creating a place of safety. These lines are the last of a somewhat long poem.

CHAPTER 6

The Hill Country

It is Persephone's tale alone that quiets him
... till she comes home the pasture all about her
she smells of Pluto of money and the darkness
and he loves her again as he loves instinct itself

—Robert Cooper, St. Bruno[13]

As long as Bob and I were living on the edges of the Texas Hill Country, we could picnic most of the year—that or just simply get out into the countryside. We walked with the ducks in Bourne, waded in the Frio below the cliffs near Leakey, and devoured Derby Pie at the Cypress Creek Café in Wimberley. Perhaps we were taken with it so because of the stark beauty of the hills and the freshness of our love for each other. We'd find some lovely spot where we could spread Bob's old, raggedy blue blanket and pop open our bottle of wine. The Blanco, Guadalupe, and Pedernales Rivers all have wonderful spots to sit and unwind. Some are quiet spots where the water flows serenely, while others, especially along the Pedernales, excited us as they ripped their way to the Gulf of Mexico. We would sometimes climb up a granite batholith called Enchanted Rock; it offered a great location from which we could enjoy vistas to the horizon, our "Elysian Fields," we would say. Here and there, we would spot a scrub oak growing up out of the rock and in its meager shade enjoy relief from the intense Hill Country sun. We would sit and rest as we gazed out into the countryside looking back toward the east. Sometimes we would be sitting in silences, long and unbroken, and at other times continue a conversation that had begun years before and that never came to an end, though its character changed, until the hour Bob fell silent at the last.

Enchanted Rock lent itself to our mystical instincts. It was said to have been held sacred by the ancient people who first climbed it, and it does possess an air of some presiding deity who was not at all pleased by hikers who were clattering about the mounded stone in a disrespectful way. The wind blew hard in response to them. We were always careful to tidy up behind ourselves and to tuck a morsel of food into some crack in the stone as an offering to this disgruntled spirit. Alfred North Whitehead had written, and Bob enjoyed quoting, "Philosophy may not neglect the multifariousness of the world—the fairies dance and Christ is nailed to the cross."[14] Never did the fairy dances seem truer than when we sat up there soaking in the beauty of it all. At the end came the full force of the multifariousness of nature, Bob's illness. Then, while we suffered, the fairies danced on paying us no heed at all.*

Bob had a fascination with mythologies in general, the mythology of the Greeks in particular. Initially, my knowledge was marginal; I had had a great time learning of it here and there over the years. There had been no system to my studies, just willy-nilly fascination. Jean Shinoda Bolen wrote a book that she entitled *Goddesses in Everywoman*, and Bob, having enjoyed reading it, bought me a copy. The next time we spoke, Bob asked me which of the goddesses I thought I most resembled. I said I thought I was most nearly represented in Persephone, the goddess captured by the god Hades and taken away to reign as queen beside him in the land of shades. Bob, thinking I was going to say Aphrodite, asked me to explain. I couldn't; it just seemed right, and as the years went by, my choice became clearer. I do now live in the land of the shades with my beloved. I never asked Bob why he thought Aphrodite would be my choice. I suppose I assumed I knew. I was always failing to ask Bob questions, tending to think I was hearing the

* This is a perfect example of the vast difference between Bob's intellect and mine. I can recall that I read a book, but Bob could quote from it. Some things he quoted enough that I could repeat it. This is one of those things. Interestingly enough, those things bore great importance in the times of nearly overwhelming stress and loss.

unspoken. I believe that most of the time I did, but there must have been much that I missed as well. He was the same way with me. We seemed to be tuned in to the same thoughts much of the time. We often marveled at this, saying that we *began* one another's sentences.

When I asked Bob to inscribe my book, he demurred. Then the next day, he handed me this poem.

You Had Said

"On some other day when the Sun
shines you can write things in my book
you found you could not say today
about how our oak tree was red
more and more till nearly the green
was gone" And I spoke of the light
in your hair such light I'd seen once before
and only then in Greece
at Delos on the dancing floor
the vintage in and my feet strong
with "wine dark wine" all their toes wet
I had raised myself up on them
And seen you—you were breathless—and seen
The goddess her hair burn the sky
Auburn first golden and red red
As evening had been at Aulis
The slap the sound the ships had made
Loosened eastward now toward home.
(Cooper)[15]

The original copy of this poem is still folded inside my book, but an inscription isn't to be found.

Our conversation often strayed to these myths, so one afternoon as we were coming down off the great stone, I came across a crack just wide enough for me to hide myself. With Hades in mind (the Romans had called him Pluto) and with all our talk of the Elysian Fields, I tucked myself into the opening while still just barely able to see Bob. He had spun quite a spell over himself, our talk about the gods and how Hades might just get himself turned about, his chariot thundering up into the Texas hills rather than the fields of Greece as he sought Persephone. Bob was apparently preoccupied with all this talk. I laugh when I recall how he looked startled for that moment when he lost sight of me, only to find me hiding behind the edge of stone. He said something about getting me out of there before Hades did show up to whisk me away. Then, in a more somber tone, he said he could not imagine his life without me. I could not imagine mine without him either.

I cannot read the poem "You Had Said" without also thinking of our days in the New England countryside and the beauty of a crisp autumn, or how with delight he introduced me to the California wine country, the coming in of the grape harvest. His poetry haunts my thoughts. He filled up my soul, still does. The poetry is a source of bliss for me and will be so as long as memory lingers.

In the early days of his illness, he had the delusion that our house traveled from place to place—usually to one of the places that had been important to us, that and North Carolina where he had been as a boy. Bob had enjoyed the beauty of the northern woods and lakes. These images often filled his poems, that and the iciness of the winters. Curiously enough, our home never set down there. I often urged him to take me there, and while he never said no, I knew that he was not going to return. It was such a part of him, the pain of him, and while I still have the yearning to go, I do not have the courage and emotional fortitude to go alone.

Eventually, our home would stop its traveling. For quite some time, he might not be completely certain where he was when he awoke in the morning. The presence of friends, particularly Lajean and Dari Hill and Patty Thompson, helped him to locate himself more easily. But he could not so readily locate himself in time. Sometimes those whom he had known as children were young again, particularly Rebecca's children. Bob often wanted to know about how Bailey was. As a little one, she had spent the greatest amount of time with us. One of my fondest memories was when we explored a quartz mine. She and Bob had scrambled down into the hole, he taking long strides down into the pit, and her spindly little legs following after. She was eight years old and had made her first plane trip alone. When it was time for her to board, we loaded her on the plane, having been allowed to accompany her to the gate. I stood at the window of the terminal looking out at her, so tiny, sitting there in her window seat. I was fighting tears, and she was too. Bob put his arm around me and suggested I take a step or two back from the window, where I would not be so easily seen. He stood in my place, waving to her, and she waved back. When the plane pushed back from the gate and he turned around, tears were streaming down his face. Later, as a young adult, she would care for him while I was recovering from surgery and he could no longer bathe or dress himself without help. But then he would forget and think she was little again. On those awful evenings, he would wake early from a frightening dream, fearing for Bailey's safety. I would assure him that all was well and that I would not go to bed until I knew she was home safely. Reassured that all was well, he would go back to bed. His fatigue would prevent him from waiting up for her with me. And his memory of that evening would have been wiped away by morning. This would be a common theme—is Bailey okay?

In those early days when she was with us, Bailey had been afraid of ghosts or intruders. She had to know how the security system worked and quickly thought of a way around it, so it was of no comfort to her. Our bedroom was in one wing of the house, and the guest rooms were across the house and past the portrait of my antebellum great-grandmother. It was disquieting for Bailey. Many evenings, Bob sat reading in his library, which was next to her room, and then, when he knew she was asleep, he would tiptoe down the hall, leaving on the light in the library. But now, in his tormented dreams, she was a little girl again and afraid; he wanted her comforted.

For those who are bewildered by his curious memory and my blatant lies, I will explain that it is a terrible mistake to try to argue or reason with someone who is in a delusional state; try to talk some sense into them, and you will irritate them further, that or humiliate them. As strange as it must sound, given his dependence upon me, Bob was still my champion, and I never wanted him humiliated by me or anyone else. It was better for me to go along and reassure him rather than rob him of his surety. If Bob said the house was moving about from North Carolina to DC to California—then the house was moving. I rather enjoyed those changes of scene. I imagined how it was to wake up to a chilly North Carolina morning again and see the dogwoods blooming. If he was fretting about not being prepared to deliver a lecture at the local university, I would offer to call ahead to see if there might be any possible changes to the schedule. After my phony phone call, I would report back that his duties had been rescheduled; this calmed him. He would sink into bed with relief. There would have been no excuse for me to assert my superior knowledge of the world by trying to tell him that he was delusional and trying to straighten him out; that could only do him harm. Within a few minutes, all would be forgotten; he would never think of that particular event again. And when he had similar concerns, I would do the same thing, knowing that he would not recall how many times lectures had been "rescheduled."

Through all this, he never forgot my name. So many suffer from the loss of recognition by their beloved, but from that we were spared. The same was true of his brother Gary and friends with whom he still had contact. The old friends never disappeared. This was one of those inexplicable islands of recall; the human brain is a most peculiar and amazing thing. I have wondered if the greatest confusion is that we often make no distinction between the brain and the mind. The brain may fail, but the mind runs on and from time to time finds a way to express itself clearly.

On some Hill Country outings, Bob and I would head for Inks Lake; it's a beautiful, small lake created by the Colorado River, where there are outcroppings of the same pink Precambrian rock as that at Enchanted Rock.* When we sat there along those rocky banks, we were loving each other and feeling as if we were both grasping, and being cradled by, the very bones of the earth. With some blurry, undefined paganism, we were caught up in enchantment by the world; here on the shores of Inks was one of those places where the mystery of it all would break through into our hearts. I would find myself going back to those times and seeking comfort there. But memories are never orderly; as I write this, I find myself thinking of a day we spent among the boulders in the Garden of the Gods outside Colorado Springs. Bob was grieving the loss of another dear friend, Taylor Stevenson. For the next several years, Bob would be weaving himself back and forth across the country, preaching at the funerals of one friend after another. When dear Will died, Bob was so grieved and so ill himself that he just sat and wept. I had never seen him grieve so profoundly before, though I wondered if it also had been this way when Terry died. Bob then told

* I refer to the Colorado that flows into the Gulf of Mexico.

me about conversations that he and Will had had that week. Ordinarily, Bob would write, and Will would not, so finally one or the other would telephone. Contact had been sporadic since we had left Texas, but oddly enough, that week they had spoken twice. Will had said his usual "Goodbye, hon," and then, just hours later, died in his sleep. Bob always claimed that in some way we all consent to our end. I wonder if Will was knowing and not knowing that his end was at hand. Why two conversations just days apart? Was he trying to tell Bob something that he could not articulate? I wonder if he was trying to say goodbye with a finality that had not been there before.

There Are Too Damned Many Ghosts Now

There are too damned many ghosts now you said
is that what it's like to get old?

But you know on which sides
of the stones and the trees
the lichens grow
all you need to know
is where you are

More and more our memories
are peopled now with the names
of the dead our friends
and if we've been anything
at all our enemies.

You can't be sure where "old"
started in just what parts
of your body, belly, mind or brain
it began but it began
you fear you become the ghosts

It is very clear very dark
sparkles here like a live
wire broken in some endless

night empty of others

Resolved the ghosts are
the foxfire gleams along
the circuits of yourself
in the woods toward the swamps
phosphorescent

gather about the fires

the vacant chairs rock
rock among the stones
among the last standing trees
shades
(Cooper)[16]

We both loved Will dearly; he was among the most creative professors, a gifted, funny man, and our dear friend. I just sat there beside Bob and cried with him as we held onto each other. When the hour of Will's funeral came, and Bob had not been well enough to make the trip back to Texas, we sat at the dining table, and Bob read the mass. Then we remembered the good times, especially the near-weekly Sunday night dinners that the three of us had enjoyed sitting together at that same table. We also recalled the evening that Will and Nancy Whitworth invited us to a play and dinner to celebrate our first wedding anniversary. I had thought at the time that they had planned an ambitious evening; our restaurants closed early in those days. When we left the theater, Will said he needed to go by his office. When we got there, Nancy hopped out with him. Bob and I glanced at our watches in the dim light. I was trying to think of what I had in the refrigerator that could be pulled together for a light supper. They were gone some time, and when they returned, they loaded a large, boxy container into the back of Will's SUV. We started out in the direction of a well-known restaurant, but just as I thought we might turn left, we turned right and stopped at the slip where Nancy's boat was moored. The now recognizable hamper went into the boat, and out we went onto a palely moonlit lake, one of those lakes strung like irregularly sized pearls along the twine of the Colorado. No sooner were we into a shielded lagoon than out came the silver, crystal, and china. There with dear friends we celebrated our first anniversary and the end of a year that had begun with the bliss of a new home, the wine country, and Boston and then ended with the pains of academic life, with Bob in the center of the maelstrom where he had knowingly put himself, even had a hand in creating. Bob and I knew, between ourselves, how we were going to end it, but everyone was going to lose something, and some were going to lose a lot. But for that lovely evening, we floated peacefully with friends who wanted to celebrate our marriage with us and to lift us out of the fray, even if for an all too brief evening. I will think forever lovingly of these two friends and the evening on the lake.

I have strayed from the Hill Country but not by far. Thinking of Will takes me back there again. Sometimes it was just Bob and I on our outings, and other times we would have other friends with us. We ate sautéed celery at a little restaurant in Fredericksburg and loads of pastries from the German bakeries across the main street from the restaurant. We were all fascinated by the authentic tea house and Japanese garden at the Nimitz Museum. Occasionally we would drive over and have something cold to drink in Luckenbach. Other times we would head out to the Vineyard's Ranch with Harriet and another of Bob's students. We would rumble around in the ranch jeep until we all had concussions from the banging about. After supper, we would fall asleep to be awoken by the trills of the canyon wrens and the idiotic attempts of the mockingbirds to mimic them. If we were headed through Marble Falls, we stopped at the Bluebonnet Cafe. In the spring, we could be found in this same area, but rather than the lakes, we wandered the bluebonnet fields—oh glory.

I recently drove through this area on my way back from a Thanksgiving holiday near Blanco, and the air was so heavy with nostalgia that I almost could not breathe. We, Bob and I, did not consciously live each day as if it were the last, but I believe we did come close to living our days to the fullest. Bob would forever remind me that there would never be enough; he was so right. There will never be enough time or full moons or the sound of water dashing over limestone, so I will drift down my ever-widening stream on the soft memory of how Bob loved me just "as he had loved instinct itself" (Cooper, St. Bruno). I find myself daydreaming of the banks of Inks and how safe I felt sitting there leaning back against Bob, his arms around me and the most ancient stone known below me.

CHAPTER 7

The Milagros

Why, who makes much of a miracle?
As to me I know of nothing else but miracles,

—Walt Whitman, "Miracles"

San Antonio had been important to me; my dear friend Lynn Schaefer and I had spent a good bit of time there as playmates—adult ones that is. It was her hometown, and I would go with her fairly often; we would call on all her friends who had shops along the River Walk. I still have a jacket and wide belts that were imported to San Antonio from Guatemala and snatched up by me while there. This was the era of hippie chicks, and Lynn was known for her Oaxacan wedding dresses shortened a bit and worn over her bell-bottoms. Later it was Bob who got me to San Antonio again. Initially he drove a VW Bug on the interstate when he traveled to San Antonio for his appointments with a psychiatrist. The traffic was making him quite anxious. I had a newer car, so I would leave my keys hidden under the floor mat, and he would stop by the lot outside my work and swap cars, leaving his keys so that I could make my way home in the afternoons. My car was small, but at least it had a roll bar, and that gave it some measure of safety beyond what his afforded. We rarely talked much about his sessions when he got back. It would not have been appropriate; besides, the trip left him exhausted. Generally he would just drop my keys off and head home. When he wanted to talk, he would and did.

Later on when I began a designing studio again, my schedule was my own. We began to explore San Antonio. It is a wonderful city and in some ways like stepping into another country. I knew the River Walk area and the Mercado. But Bob and I found another little area out on the loop. There we came upon some wonderful pottery and a good Mexican restaurant as well as an import shop that sold the most magnificent *milagros,* crude wooden crosses, encrusted with miniature arms, hands, legs, hearts, dogs, angels, and a sun with rays—all sorts of things. Milagros translates to miracles in Spanish, and the tin fetishes represent things that the supplicant might pray for. We bought two, one for ourselves and one to take with us the next time we visited Ernest.

We enjoyed the River Walk, its boats and restaurants. We also were people watchers and would sometimes sit in the amphitheater and rest while we watched families mill around as people will. There were, beyond the amphitheater, small houses that had been converted into shops where artists and craftspeople sold their wares. It was here that Bob bought a magenta punch bowl that he treasured. Whether any of these landmarks remain I do not know. If they do not, I do not want to be told.

I learned a hard lesson the only time I spent some lonely, sad hours in those old environs after Bob's passing. I had not been to Texas at all during the ten years that Bob had been homebound. When I returned, I spent much of my day alone, going to all of the places where I had lived and most especially to the places where Bob and I had been together. It was not that locations had changed so much as it was that they no longer offered entrance to me. I had a meeting scheduled, and I had arrived there the evening before and gone by the seminary. It was spring break, and I saw not one soul. Dust and leaves had blown up around the door into the vestibule from which Bob's office had opened. The chapel had been turned sideways so that half the chairs faced away from the bronze cross that was outside the glass wall that served as a reredos. The pulpit from which Bob had preached now had half of the chairs turned away from it, the same with the altar. Our oak tree was hemmed in by new construction. But worst of all, Bob's door was locked against me. And yet, if I could have walked in, how horrible that would have been. It would have been void of his books, the rocker, and his desk set up on two-by-four boards to make room for his knees.

When I went by our apartments, I found that they were fresh and blue. Gone were the earth tones of our era. Again precious-dog-Charlie and I got out and walked about where Bob and I had gone, but we could not go up those steps and walk in to find Bob there. The appointment that I had driven down early for was canceled the next morning, but fool that I am, I did it again, except this time I added the apartment where Lynn had lived. Someone had done what I had dreamed of doing, turning the upper and lower apartments into a single home. Again it was painted blue and lovely, but I no longer had the key, and Bob would not be stopping by to visit us in front of the fire. Last of all, I went to the condo that we had bought as our first home together. It was not for sale, but I knew via Zillow that it was rental property now. I pulled up into the driveway, toying with the idea of making an offer on it. I could not see if the peach tree that we had planted had survived without us to tend to it. But reality has to have its way. A younger couple living in a three-story condo is one thing, but now it would be absurd to start over that way. Over the years of wondering where home was, I had thought of our first home and tried to think how to put an elevator in, but that was all magical thinking. Once again, I had no key, just the bittersweetness of it all. My friends were all scattered; most were in the various suburbs. Some had gone to Santa Fe, Harry and Charla among them. This city had been home. I had gone there when I was eighteen to enroll in the university and stayed until after I married Bob, but I did not belong there anymore. I quit making myself miserable, backed down the driveway, and headed to the Hill Country; there I did belong. There the memories are all sweet ones. There had never been doors in the "wild" that could be locked against us—no meanness—no gossips—just the two of us and the beauty of the earth. My ghost and I wandered about with smiles on our faces. An added gift received since those earlier days is the presence of my daughter and granddaughter, Melissa, and her family—all now living in the hills. Now I found hugs and love and understanding. It had been a hard trip and an even harder lesson.

I took walks along the ridge, and my thoughts returned to sweet times. Somewhere along the way, Bob and I had abandoned the interstate and began driving to San Antonio on the Hill Country roads. We would pack a lunch and eat it in the car on the way. One time I had bought a bad piece of Brie. Bob had taken a big bite off the end, and just as the horror of it registered with my taste buds, Bob was spitting his out the window and tossing the remaining chunk out behind. That all happened over the Blanco River. From then on, when we drove over that bridge, we looked for some ever-increasing hole that the cheese had gnawed into the asphalt. Why is it that lovers can find something funny in the silliest things? They do. It is easy for lovers to entertain themselves. When Bob fell ill, I missed that until I discovered it was still there if I would adjust myself to a different kind of humor.

One of my best memories of San Antonio was our trip over one night to see a performance of the *Nutcracker*. It was a lovely evening despite the bitter cold. For decades, we never missed seeing a performance no matter where we were, until Bob was too crippled to go. By that time, we had seen it danced by many different companies. That night in San Antonio, we also saw a woman in a beautiful white fur, ballerina-length cape. It was beautiful. Bob spent the next twenty years or more looking for something similar. He did find a long fur coat; I was delighted to have it, but the greatest joy for me was his pleasure when it first came off the hanger and I put it on. He loved beautiful things, and he made me feel beautiful. When he was ill and I would go in to say good morning, he would invariably say, "I love you, and you are beautiful." I asked myself if, when he was gone, I could continue to speak encouragingly to myself without his support. Well, yes and no. It sure was better when he did it—and with him, it did not seem to ever matter whether or not I was pulled together. He saw with eyes of love. If ever I said something about being older, Bob would quote Yeats, "But one man loved the pilgrim soul in you, / And the sorrows of your changing face" ("When You Are Old").

So what were the miracles?* There have been so many. The first and greatest was that we were ever together at all. We were among the most stubborn of people, and each had been determined to be married for life; we had always known that of each other and admired and encouraged it in each other. It took mighty upheavals to shake either one of us free from the determination to keep that marital vow, no matter what. But there did come mighty disruptions indeed, ones that very nearly destroyed both of us by different means. Thoughts of the preference of suicide over divorce had occurred to each of us, though we never spoke of it to each other, in our times of crisis. In that era, clergy faced cruel judgments, heightened by self-condemnation. So that we ever made our way to each other astonished us. I think of Edith Wharton's line from *Ethan Frome*, "They seemed to come suddenly upon happiness as if they had surprised a butterfly in the winter woods."

The second miracle was that the luster of our romance never completely wore off. It had to be buffed back to a shine from time to time, but we remained deeply in love. Each of us was married to the most interesting person we knew, and that is something that filled us with awe and gratitude. The third miracle was that our sexual appetites were generally the same, except for those times when fatigue overwhelmed. When fatigued or anxious, Bob juiced himself up again through his sexuality, and I thought he had lost his mind because I went to ground when tired. But those times were never beyond our ultimate comprehension, compassion for each other, and determination to find a way. The realization of what was happening and the willingness to compromise are what got us through; however, it remained an issue until we sat down and analyzed what was going on and when it was that we would find ourselves at odds, because we had not always been

---

* I have no interest in defining what I mean by miracles. As an undergraduate, I sat about for four years debating with fellow students and our professors about what art is—only to come to the conclusion that I'll know art when I see it. I'm not interested in definitions—never was, unless it furthered my cause in a game of one-up-womanship/manship. Miracles are like art; they can only be defined by the recipient of one, and you know it when you experience it, if you care to. What is my miracle may not be yours. My dear, charming professor of theology, William Green, must be turning in his grave at that. But he knew the day he asked me if I believed in the virgin birth and I said, "No, but check back with me again on Christmas Eve," that I was incorrigible.

that way. Once we named what was happening, it was within our control to manage. I have seen too many marriages crack apart at this very point.

Perhaps this is not a miracle, but it was a happy commonality. We could be content to sit side by side and read for hours. We guarded each other's privacy and understood the need for solitude. After Bob stopped traveling, he was ubiquitous, and I was overwhelmed with the absence of solitude. I recall speaking of this to Lynn, but she—who lived alone and claimed she did not like it—had no sympathy for me. So I told Bob, and Friday afternoons became the time we maintained silence in our home. That fell away when Bob no longer knew Mondays from Fridays or any other day, but he napped often, and that gave me a chance to breathe.

And more? There was the beauty of our homes that grew more elaborate over time as pieces were inherited from our families. There was the mass of friends before Bob's illness and the steadfastness of some during it. I have undertaken an impossible task—this business of enumerating the goodness of the Almighty. But there are some things that are so fresh in my mind that I am compelled to name them. These are the answers to my specific prayer—those times when I encountered what Bob referred to in *Engaging the Spirit* as "the always-coming-upon-us God—who continually illumines us, both dwelling *upon* us and dwelling *among* us"[17] (p. 71).

Daughter Rebecca and I had crafted the prayer primarily while sitting out on the terrace the summer that Bob's decline became a precipitous one. Either face-to-face or on the phone, she and I worked on the prayer through those months, making sure that we were clear in what we were asking. In the end, the answers to this prayer that I had prayed every morning were direct and specific. For example, Bob was never touched by other than loving hands, and I lived long enough to see him to his parting. Additionally, he was able to stay at home to the end, and also I was present at his passing. The most important of the miracles was that Bob was taken before dementia had completely overtaken him. So many miracles—precious, faith-confirming miracles. I am filled with hope for the future. And that is a miracle too. I am also not afraid—what a deliverance! In the end, Bob's body simply began to shut down, and having said goodbye to those he loved, he slipped quietly away.

I can only wonder at what the skeptic might be thinking now. How could I talk about miracles when Bob was so horribly stricken and I have seen so much loss over my lifetime? There is no life in which there has been no sadness and grief, or if there is such a life, I do not want to live it. I can only imagine that the one longing for such a life is not realizing that without some sorrow, there comes a stagnation and barrenness—a hollowness of soul—that is hideous to contemplate. So long as there are some good times—some relief here and there—I am capable of finding meaning in the painful. It is also true that I do not want to limit the power of God to what we were given, because there are so many who are blessed in other ways. I do not want to do harm to those who must, as a part of their pilgrimage, go all the way to the end of dementia with their loved ones. I can only hope that you too keep your eyes open for the miracles that are yours and are nothing like those that were granted to us. The Almighty is in all things.

Not long before his death, Bob said to me, "Annie, I was going to change the world." In so many ways, he did. He certainly changed mine. When he was a toddler, his parents took him to the North Carolina shore. As he looked out at the Atlantic Ocean, he said, "Mop, mop!" What was true of him as a toddler was true as an adult. The work was massive, but not until the end did he realize it was beyond completion. He had labored on. He had worked his brain and intellect with such fervor, with such an intense desire to make the world a better place, that, in the end, he set his brain on fire. But before he flamed out, I believe that I saw him find peace in knowing that he had done what he could. I understood his remark to be one of reflection, not regret. His mind and heart were tired and in need of rest. Longfellow wrote in a poem entitled "My Lost Youth":

> And the burden of that old song,
> It murmurs and whispers still;
> 'A boy's will is the wind's will,
> And the thoughts of youth are long long thoughts.'

But Bob was ready to give up those long thoughts of perfection; it was a lesson at which he had had a prolonged struggle. When he was able to give up that idealistic, quixotic illusion, he was ready to go.

I believe the following poem to be one of the most beautiful that Bob wrote. The idea for it came to him when we were walking along the beach in

Carpinteria, where I/we lived on the weekends and summer sessions while I was working on my doctorate. It is prophetic and gives my reader some sense of how he approached his end and how he saw the loss of purpose. Though when this was written, we could not have known how it would all end.

Patmos

"The taste of you we have on our tongues.
Each stone came from the father stone."
Bruno

John has begun again to gather stones
Though no one told him to do it this time.
There was no vision as before, no bone-
Deep knowledge and nothing at all sublime

Had happened. He had gone for a walk alone
On the beach. This is not how it once was
Back then when the Sun in a focused cone
Fell and circled him when the eagle's claws

Were solid in his back. There was no pain.
Light and voice became one thing one vast buzz.
The ocean in his ears, the salt clasped
Him into silence he'd not heard again

Since the diaphanous golden womb-days.
God had not told him. The eagle had not.
Released after how long he came to gaze
Back at where his question began to plot

Its own course. He had gathered a small store
Of the sea-washed stones but scarcely saw
Anything special in them. He added more
And more one at a time now after the claw

Of the eagle opened and set him back
On the beach. One eye he keeps on the sky
In these days when all his purpose grew slack
And left him to think this: There is no *why*

Do I do this still? Build stones of silence
And work on till the gone God relents.
(Cooper)[18]

Bob worked on at some mysterious work. He did it in patience and increasing silence, and when that work was done, the "gone-God" relented and let him move homeward at last. His work was done; he knew it, and I knew it as well. I certainly did not think of him as having an incomplete life. It was and is hard to let him go, but he was done—bless his soul, his faithful soul. He had always been heroic in his rascally sort of way, and he was to the end.

After his death, I found a note he had written to himself and placed in a drawer in his library. It is in a hand that shows he had penned it before the illness was too terribly advanced. I cannot, for all my trying, find the source. In the upper corner of the note is written "P. Burke" and below that "p. 192." In the body of the page is the word Tansillo, followed by four lines of Italian. Below that is what appears to be Bob's translation, "This man aspired to the stars, and if he did not reach them, it was life and not ardor which gave out." I believe this to be another indication of how Bob was coming to terms with the inability to finish what he would have liked to do. But then who could have? He had set his sights so terribly high. We are such frail creatures, and no one of us can do much of anything alone.*

Among the arms and legs, eyes and hearts on the milagros, there is no human brain.

---

* I have made every attempt to locate the source of this quotation and have failed. There may not be any relationship among the things entered there. I have used it, nonetheless, because it helps me, and perhaps my reader, find what Bob was thinking and how he was processing what was happening to him as dementia laid claim to his brain. Including the contents of the note seemed integral to our story.

CHAPTER 8

The Sabbatical

You meant it for evil,
But God meant it for good

—Genesis 50:20*

Just a few weeks after returning from our honeymoon, we were off for Bob's sabbatical. We had arrived in Boston for the heat of its summer, but when Labor Day arrived, it was as if a switch had been thrown somewhere. We enjoyed lovely fall days when we could pack a lunch and eat it out on the Commons near the lake. There were boats for hire, and we laughed as we watched people trying to maneuver them about. It was a far cry from the rowers sitting backward in their shells as they sculled through the water of the Charles River just a few blocks away. It was in the Commons where we could listen to the laughter of children—something that we never heard in our brownstone. There were children sitting on the bronze ducklings, lovers lying on blankets, students reading in the shade, and people like us sitting or strolling about, watching it all. It was a wonderful way to escape a small apartment, and we felt lucky that we lived only a couple of blocks away from this lovely place. Every weekday, I would leave our apartment and make a trip across the Commons with my shopping bag on my way to DeLucas

* Translated by AH-C.

Grocery, where I would do some urban foraging before making the trip back again. Each time, I would gather more than we needed and save it for the weekend or for slushy days when I did not want to go out.

We had come to the Back Bay section of Boston on the advice of a friend, Terry Maltsburger, a physician and psychoanalyst. He and Bob had met while serving on some committee for the national church. Terry had arranged for Bob to study as a fellow at the Boston Psychoanalytic Institute. He had also introduced Bob to a Jesuit friend who was a psychoanalyst, physician, and professor at Boston College. Bob would study at the Institute and coteach at the college. He was elated with the plan. I was more subdued. Having just begun to get my designing studio off the ground, I would now be abandoning it for the next six months. I had no clue what I would do with myself once there, but then Boston displayed all her delights.

There is a compactness to Boston that made possible walking to almost anywhere we wanted to go, and when walking was not a possibility, the T was there. The Museum of Fine Arts has an art school where folks like me could enroll on a short-term basis. I had always wanted to study watercolor; I had also been told that it was one of the most difficult medium to master. I've never liked to start things at which I was not pretty sure I could do passably well, and watercolor had been described as something "nearly impossible." This had been said by fellow students when I was an undergraduate—questionable sources at best. Nevertheless, I thought being 1,700 miles from home gave me a fairly good margin of error, so I enrolled. That opened a world of unexpected delight for me. I took to it immediately; when not in class, I would be painting on our dining table that we had shoved up against the window so I could get the light. It was frustrating that I would lose natural light so early on in the fall afternoons; I was captivated and could have painted forever if I had had the proper light in which to do it. It is puzzling to me that with Bob's diagnosis, I would set down my brush; I have been unable to paint ever since. I would like for the urge to return, but I never felt as if it were mine to keep, because the forms that took shape in front of me never seemed to have found their source in me. I have heard other painters say similar things, but a dry time as long as this leaves me to wonder if I will ever paint again. That is certainly no loss to the world, but it is a loss to me. I keep brushes and paint at ready.

When not painting or shopping at DeLucas, I would shop at the green grocers on the edges of the North End, but those men were so audacious that I soon learned to go only when Bob was with me. We also began a practice of buying fresh, cut flowers every week. In Boston, it was orchids that were sold on the street; in Florida, it would be gladiolas; and now it is roses but not on Little Rock streets. We did find that we could pick our own daffodils here if we drove out to Wye Mountain, but that lasts only for the month of March. So roses it is—not much of a sacrifice! My favorites are pinkie peach or maybe white in the winter, but Bob favored the yellow rose. We would buy what we could find and put them in the crystal rose bowl that we found in Dunedin's little downtown.

Terry made Bostonians of us. He arranged for us to have entrance to the Athenæum during our stay in Boston. Bob and I went every Thursday afternoon for tea. We would browse around the archives and enjoy watching in action some of the most charmingly eccentric people I have ever met. One of them, a frail wisp of a woman, regularly wore two large watches on her tiny wrist and rubber-soled, China-made Mary Janes on her feet. There must have been a wonderful story to have been told by that person, and had I been in the South, I would have known how to politely trigger its telling, but this was reserved Boston. I have had to content myself with conjuring up countless options to tell myself about her.

Terry didn't stop with the Athenæum; he introduced us to wonderful friends, entertaining us in his home on Beacon Hill or at the Summerset Club. He also took us to restaurants where the locals went. Our first afternoon there, we were led through the curving streets off the main path to an Italian restaurant. It was midafternoon, and parked immediately outside the entrance was a black Cadillac with windows as dark as the car itself; the engine was running. I was absolutely certain that the restaurant was on the verge of being pelted with bullets from a machine gun. Apparently seeing *Walk East on Beacon Street* as a kid had made quite an impression on me.

Bob and I spent Saturdays walking in the North End, which had some of our favorite destinations. I enjoyed the smell of salt air, the Italian pastries, and a butcher's shop with the rabbits hanging by their feet in the window. And, oh happy day, Bob found a liquor store that carried George Dickel; now Bruce would no longer have to ship it to him in a box labeled "Figurine." Paul Revere's house had also been a thrill—crooked walls and low, sagging ceilings. Bob had to stoop way over and finally left me to do the tour by myself when things became impossibly low for him. I chided him for not just slithering through on his belly. I have a photo of him stretched out on the tomb of one of the Mathers, Increase or Cotton I recall not; Bob is supported only from his knees to his shoulders, with his hat resting on his chest and his head held in his hands. Then, of course, there was the delight of Old North Church, coming upon it suddenly and unexpectedly.

On our way back home, we could stop at Filene's Basement, where Bob held my coat, shielding me from view as I tried on clothes. I had been an art major and was not too worried about who saw me in my underwear, but it clearly mattered to him. While in Boston, we bought a tux for Bob at a swanky men's shop. You can only imagine the complete bewilderment and then consternation of the tailor when Bob wanted the pants hemmed so that he could wear them with his good dress boots. Well, what else would you wear with your tux in Texas, or Florida, or New Jersey, or Arkansas, or on a cruise? I have seen Bob in black patent lace-ups and white tie, but that was in New Orleans where the Krewe had fashion police at the door—curious that those balls were almost as bawdy as Euripides's "Kyklops" and at the same time so stern about sartorial matters. I am a student of the unending paradoxes of individuals and their institutions. I hope I never come to say that I have seen it all, because it can't possibly be true. Perhaps that is why I still continue practicing psychotherapy. I remain astonished by human beings and the polymorphous perversity of it all, as Freud would have put it. I am too intrigued by people to tire of them; we are fascinating creatures.

One day, when messing around on the far side of the Charles River, Bob and I raced to the top of Bunker Hill and nearly died there. Another day while wandering about, we saw some beautiful frigates that had been commissioned long ago. They were tall and stately and must have been majestic when their sails were unfurled. One was, we were told, Ol' Ironsides. I hope that was true; I'd like to be able to say I had seen it. We wandered around Harvard Square and stopped for calamari sushi that I would still be chewing if I had not decided to discretely leave it behind. Once we caught the train and went up to Salem so that I could see the Witch House and the House of Seven Gables. I was in heaven; these were the things that had fascinated me since childhood, and here I was. I had grown up in Texas where so many things were new when compared to this.

A Red Panther for Rembrandt Bugati

"They would have burned you as a witch"
he told you "if you'd lived in another age"
You did where the water is shallow at the river's
edge or still there is ice for longer than we know
and fossils too for eyes very old at seeing
since all the earth's great stones were liquid fire once
rivers that settled themselves into families

We are looking for the time when we were everything we are
We are looking for the time before we were anything
He doesn't know you came from one of them
Or let the colors melt your primitive soul down
drain and drip to the border of the canvas
that violent frame of discourse be
your single answer *your* word be

Then if he will paint you
hang and leave for the gallery's myriad eyes
you won't be there
(Cooper)[19]

Sometimes I was not sure which of us was more thrilled, me seeing all these things I had studied and read about or Bob watching my pleasure in all of this; he had brought me to a good place, and he was aware of that. It is wonderful to be loved like that; it creates such a sense of freedom within, a feeling that is still with me. While work was being done by both of us, this was primarily a time of playfulness. We would return to grief in Texas. Not until we got to Florida, almost a year later, did the real fun begin again. We were lovers, yes, but as much as that, we were playmates. When I think of it, lovemaking and playing have many of the same characteristics, or should.

On Sunday mornings, we attended various Boston churches; we even were called in as Christian ed consultants at Trinity. Prior to seminary, I had been working at a large parish where I oversaw a faculty of eighty, and, of course, Bob was well versed in the education of adults. But Trinity was too big for us—literally; I couldn't see well enough to see the altar! We also went to church with Terry at Advent, but ultimately we settled in at Emmanuel. It was an exquisitely beautiful and lush, if well-worn, church tucked into a nook on Newberry Street. The music was particularly fine, and the preacher was prophetic. One cannot ask for more. After services, we went around the corner to drink our lunch at the bar in the Ritz Hotel. Well, not just drink; they had the most wonderful sugared nuts that we loved. Then off for a Sunday-afternoon nap. It was when walking home for one of those naps that I said to Bob that someone ought to write a dissertation on a particular topic. As it turned out, that someone was I.

The time in Boston that most stands out in my mind was the Thanksgiving there. Bob had thought more about it than had I. Our apartment was small and simple but charming, in a shabby sort of way, with a reasonably well-fitted kitchen. I guess I thought I would cook, but Bob made reservations for us at the Parker House Hotel. We had selected the late seating. The hotel is a beautiful one with rich wood paneling everywhere and brocade at the windows. In the dining room, the service was courteous and unhurried. We just savored each course. That day, I was introduced to pumpkin soup. I loved it, and from that Thanksgiving, until Bob's passing, pumpkin soup was on the menu in our home. After a leisurely dinner, we began the walk back to our brownstone. The sun was rolling along the horizon. The light on the Commons was breathtakingly beautiful, as if someone had come and sprinkled fairy dust on everything, and the low sun left you nearly blinded by the glory. It seemed we had the world to ourselves as we strolled along. I was snuggled in my coat with my arm in Bob's. I was never, never happier than when I was nestled against him. His height and strength were always a source of comfort to me; he made me feel safe. We were so in love and so happy. We were at peace. Sometimes there are those magical times that play out themselves over and over again in your mind and heart. That afternoon is one of those; my mind has returned to sights and sensations of that day time and again over the years. Its memory is a source of comfort and pleasure and strength that helped power me through the darker days of Bob's illness, and even now. Today I feast on the dearness of that afternoon just as we had feasted on turkey and rolls and pumpkin soup that day.

Our dear friend Lynn came to see us and introduced us to some friends of hers who had a second home on Cape Cod. At Christmastime, they took us to Nantucket—a little fairyland in the winter, perhaps year-round. The cobbled streets, almost deserted at that time of year, were decorated with cedar trees covered with ornaments made from aluminum pie tins. We walked about the island enjoying, in the quiet, the charming nineteenth-century houses, stopping now and then for coffee or hot soup along the way. At one point, we were surprised by coming upon an open house at the Jared Coffin House. It was decorated for the holidays according to its period. We were welcomed in and offered tea and cookies by men and women in period dress; they and the house were charming. The island seemed nearly deserted, so I have often wondered whom they were expecting to have made such an effort. Perhaps they did it as much for themselves as for anyone. That's a good enough reason for doing something—doing it because it gives you pleasure and helps bring order to your world. It holds on to tradition. The first fall after Bob's death, I almost did not put out fall decorations as had been our custom. As I stood in the living room looking out the bay window, I could have sworn I heard Bob's voice speak to me: "Don't disappoint me by letting yourself down." I raced into the attic to retrieve the boxes and decorated for fall! I have decorated for every season since, even if I am very nearly the only one who knows it.

When it was time for the last ferry to leave Nantucket, we boarded it with a yearning to return to that island and its jewel box of a town—something we never did. I would never be more grateful for my snuggly coat than on that day, especially when we were ferried back and forth between Hyannis and Nantucket. Except for lunch and the tea party at the Jared Coffin House, everything we had eaten or drunk that day had been sold to us by outdoor vendors, and we had sat at wooden picnic tables along the waterfront as though it were the height of summer season.

It was while in Boston working as a fellow at the Psychoanalytic Institute that Bob decided he had grown weary of academia. He wanted to begin work as a psychotherapist, and in a short time, that is what he did. Bob had been an academic since he was in his twenties, serving as chaplain and teaching in both private and public settings. He was such an extraordinary teacher that it was hard for me to believe he was done with it. I questioned him, and he persuaded me that he wanted to treat mental illnesses. Despite his tiredness with academic squabbles, upon returning to the seminary, he threw himself into a conflict that was already underway. It was over something that Bishop Benitez, who was chairman of the board of trustees, was promoting and that the faculty was opposed to. I was there when a fellow professor took Bob aside and asked him to lead them in stopping the trustees from being persuaded to vote in favor of the proposal. The rationale was that because Bob's Letter Dimissory was not in Texas, he had protection. (Others had the same protection too.) The next argument was that Bob was tenured. (Others had both external Letters Dimissory and tenure.) Finally came the real reason—Bob had the courage to do it. Courage or fool-heartedness, I am not sure which, but I do know that he was a provocateur.

The issue revolved around the required taking of vows that would be particularly punitive to gay and lesbian students and faculty. In the past, Bob had been conservative and slow (in my opinion) in coming around with regard to homosexuality, but he had thought and read and listened himself into a reversal of his view. Bishop Benitez was where Bob had been, and now it was the bishop who was wrong headed, and Bob goaded him at every turn, even to the point of, as one student put it, "scolding the bishop from the pulpit." I am sure the bishop would have heard it that way, had he deigned to be there. But it had not occurred to me when I heard the sermon that Bob was scolding. I had simply heard the Gospel, and the Gospel is not always "good news" when it goes against one's desires.

It had happened that Bob's week to be priest in charge of the ordering of services and to preach on Thursday fell on the same Thursday that the board was to meet and vote on the proposal. Members of the board were in chapel to hear what was said. Later in the day, the proposal was defeated. Word got back to "the bishop" about Bob's sermon, and he was reported to be enraged by what Bob had done. I was both proud of Bob and shocked by the realization of the consequences. I knew that Benitez would make Bob miserable, and Bob would do the same to Benitez until we left. These were men who did not know how to lose. This animosity had been enflamed even more by two things. First was Bob's scorch-the-earth manner, especially when the innocent have no voice, or could have had their aspirations destroyed if they used it. The second was that Bob had divorced and remarried beyond the bishop's reach and authority.

Bob likely would have been described as angry by those who heard the sermon; he was not. He would be later, but on that day, he was passionate. I have been asked if I was angry with Bob. I was shocked by what I knew would be the consequences. But I was not angry with him because I knew that Bob needed to move away to get out of the quagmire. We had even talked about his desire to leave Texas years before when I was a student. Had I thought he would never do it? Maybe. But it was going to be hard to leave friends and family behind; that was a tender place for me, for both of us. I still have a sadness when I think of what all we missed as the little ones grew up, but a delight at what we gained—both of us.

Bob's job may have been secure, but friendships were not; most of the faculty agreed with Bob, but they did not want to be in conflict with the board of trustees and most particularly with its chairman. They took Bob to task. Bob had carried the water, and now he was largely isolated. Few colleagues came to his defense, though some few brave ones did; and the faculty member who had approached Bob for help that night was not among his defenders. The bishop was furious and doing everything he could to "rid himself of this troublesome priest." Those had been the words of Henry VIII spoken about Thomas Moore, the priest who was ultimately beheaded. Bob managed to escape with his head intact. That spring, Bob was fighting to stay when I reminded him that he didn't want to be there. I suspected that if we just waited until the beginning of the fall semester, we could get a sizable settlement for his agreeing not to show up for opening services or to meet his classes. The plan worked, and with the proper investment, that money grew to be a quite sizable sum. But Bob was hurt terribly by all of it. Once again, he had spoken truth to power and paid the price. But in the end, it was that money and its earnings that made it possible for Bob to be cared for at home to the day of his death. Good can come from evil when the Divine is in the mix.

When I look back over Bob's life, I find that time has proven him to have come down on the side of the angels. He was right about civil rights, he was right about the ordination of women, and he was right about the place of gays and lesbians in the church. At the end, he was pretty bunged up and yearned for the quiet of therapeutic work. It had been said of Bob during the struggle for the ordination of women that he did not read his hate mail; he weighed it. But Bob was weary with the fight. He now would fight, if that is the word, alongside souls struggling to find their way back to mental health. He was a wonderful therapist, perhaps even better than professor, and that is saying a great deal. And the teaching never stopped, except that now we did it together in the parish.

He was hired immediately in a mental health clinic, as he looked forward to a full-time position somewhere else. Bob had developed an aversion to Texas that would affect the course of my life as well. Part of coming to grips with Bob's fatal illness was the struggle in me about finding home; it had been where Bob was. But when he was gone, what then? Texas with one daughter, or Colorado with the other? That struggle went on for more than a year after Bob's death, when one afternoon, as I sat down at the desk in my study looking out onto the terrace, these words came so powerfully to me, almost as if they had been spoken aloud: "You are home." With that conviction, my view of so many things changed. I began to be more responsive to old friends, the few of them who had stuck with me through Bob's illness. No, I don't like the way that sounds because it makes it sound as though the fault was not mine. I had been abandoned by some friends because I had been so thoroughly neglectful of them; I had neither accepted nor extended invitations. But some friends were not deterred, and it was to them that I reached out for company—friends like Robbie Bradford, who had been one of the first people I met upon moving here. I had rented office space from her and for the next twelve years worked in the same building. Robbie was not deterred by my hesitation to go out; she stayed after me or brought food to me.

Now though, I reconnected with old friends and also began to make new ones. Church stopped simply being only a place to which I fled for the solace of the sacraments; it also became a place where I could begin to function again, participate in its common life. The process has been painfully slow, but as I began to rebuild my life, life began to rebuild me. I miss Bob terribly, I always will, but I have the sense of his presence pressing me forward into the future. He is so much a part of me now that wherever I go, he will be there.

I began praying for friends with whom I would be at home intellectually. A few months later, a woman about my age came to sit by me in the pew. She had on a vintage hat and handbag that made her look like the late queen mother. She was Bobby, and as I got to know her, she made me think of my version of a grown-up Scout from *To Kill a Mocking Bird*. Bobby would tell you that she had not gotten around to doing that—growing up, that is. She has a blazing intellect as well as being a wild woman who can make me laugh like few others. Not long after this, we were joined by a tall, thin, willowy, glamorous blond, a lady, with the emphasis on lady. What a threesome! I love these women. What drew us together initially was the discovery that we had all suffered a terrible loss. Bobby's loss had been longer ago than Linnie's or mine, but it had been terrible and deep, yet her survival seemed to help us through the knot hole of acute grief. These two women have a sharpness of intellect and the ability to laugh and play that I had longed for and lost in losing Bob. We don't go out often, because we don't just laugh, we scream with laughter. Mostly we just gather here at headquarters (my house) and carry on until we are too tired to do it any longer. Recently when Bobby was terribly ill, I found that cloying feeling in my throat that comes with the realization that death could pull my life apart all over again. I want these women with me for a long time. But there will never be enough with them either. Nor will there be with my sister. When we were children, I, as the older sister, was lording it over her, pointing out that my age made me superior. I was taken aback at her saying, "Yeah, and you will die before me too." I forgot to ask her if that was a promise. I cannot imagine my life without her either.

I was still in a fragile state. I asked myself what gave me joy, and the answer that came back was singing the hymns in church. I began asking around for a voice teacher, and I was told to go to Linda Austin. The first time I met her was in her studio where she taught UALR students. We made arrangements for lessons. In my time with her, wonderful things began to happen to me. The songs were show tunes, often the ones my mother had sung when I was a child. As I sang, the pain began to roll out, mostly in the form of tears. Memories were being brought to mind as I sang, and Linda was always willing to listen to them. Those hours singing flew by. My lessons were at her home—a haven of creativity where I felt embraced by a wonderful warmth. It was like being wrapped in a cocoon of artistry and healing. Soon we were the dearest of friends. Though our lessons were interrupted by back surgeries that would inhibit my ability to get the necessary muscles working again, we have pressed on. When I have been ready to lose hope in myself, she has encouraged me, insisting that we sing until I was too tired to continue. At that point, we would spend the remaining time with cups of tea. Here I was again being offered tea by a teacher I admired. Linda and her husband, Bill, have helped me with the things that I have been unable to do on my own. They have helped me get Christmas to look like Christmas, and Bill has fixed all sorts of things that have needed attention. I love these people, and I feel loved by them. Taking those lessons is one of the greatest sources of healing I have found. Another source of healing has been writing. The grace of the arts, cherished friends, and the soothing beauty of the home I shared with Bob have saved me.

As Bob moved toward the end of his life, Bishop Benitez was one of the people whom Bob seemed to have forgotten ever existed. The enmity between the two men had been terrible. At one point, Bob and I had driven to Houston so that Bob could apologize for having offended the bishop so profoundly in the process of their disagreement. They had both believed themselves to be right, but it had gone beyond that. Bob wanted to try to clear the air between them—agree to disagree. But the bishop was still too angry for that. After Bob's death, I found in his Prayer Book a photo of this man. Bob truly wanted to get things right; he must have been praying himself into a place of grace. That was Bob; under it all—all the shenanigans, all the passion for causes, all the scatological language—he was given over to God. I am not saying that he did not have times of great doubt. But he always said that there is nothing worth believing that does not bring with it times of great misgivings. And it would seem that he was, through the grace of God, able to both forgive and then seemingly forget the bishop. This also seemed to be the case with all those people with whom he had unresolved conflict—he had forgotten them. It was as if they never existed—no anger, no grudges. In the end, Bob had become the person he always wanted to be—a man who let go of the unhappy parts of his past and just loved God, unencumbered.

As for me, when we got home from Boston, I resumed my design work and then picked it up again and moved it to Florida. I did that work until back problems made me decide that I needed work in which I could stand and walk rather than sit. It was that terrible back, and the struggle to recover, that sent me to work in the Morton Plant Cancer Center. That was a major turning point in my professional life. My supervisor, Meta Gustafson, is, to this day, one of my dearest friends. She lives in Maine now, but even so, since Bob's death, she has come and checked on me; she even tended to me following a recent back surgery. We talked almost nightly, one heart calling to another. Once again, as with Bob at the seminary, and then with my terrible pain, something that seemed so bad turned around and became a source of great joy. Bob became executive director of a mental health clinic sponsored by the Diocese of Southwest Florida. Along with administrative responsibilities and fundraising, he worked as a psychotherapist, treating people who were often ill with debilitating disorders as well as those who wanted to grow emotionally and spiritually. He was also associate priest at the Church of the Ascension in Clearwater, where we made countless friends. Bob was in the pulpit to his heart's content, and the rector, Dick Cobbs, was one of those strong personalities who could be in Bob's company without insecurities crippling the relationship. It was there at Ascension where Bob and I would coteach. We did that for years and loved every moment of it. Our class members never enjoyed it more than when Bob and I came down on the opposite side of things.

My work at the hospital gave me dear friends and pulled me toward a career that I find delight in to this day. Although not always perfectly, Bob and I have loved each other for better and for worse. We have loved in sickness and in health. But death has not pulled us apart; his presence with me is palpable. I have been asked, knowing now what would come, if I would have done it all over again. The answer is a loud, loud yes. There were wonderful times and hard ones, but the blessings of our marriage have never stopped. They still go on. We lived in a rain of mercies even, or perhaps I should say, especially in the hard times.

CHAPTER 9

The Poverty of Desire

What you think; you become.

—Buddha

In a recent letter, Joanie wrote of her memories and included her permission to publish the following words:

> I recall the first time we [meaning she and Ernest] visited you in Little Rock. Perhaps the first time I met the two of you. You and Ernie retired early and Bob and I sat in the kitchen talking for hours about the two of you—how you met, when love occurred, what life was like together. My memory says that his occurred one day after chapel when you passed by him as you left and touched his arm asking if everything was alright with him. He said that was when he knew there was and would be something very special between you.

I do remember that occasion but only because Bob would refer to it later and thanked me for paying attention. Otherwise I would have never given it a thought; it was such an ordinary thing, just a way of saying hello. I had touched him because he was speaking with others, and I did not want to become an interruption. I had said two words, "You okay?" Was that when he wrote "Panther"? Or did he write it much later? I do not know. I do know that I realized with that poem that we were not where we had been, and I was stunned; but for that matter, I cannot recall just when marriage became a part of our conversation either. I don't recall that he ever proposed; we just seemed to grow into all of that in an unselfconscious kind of way. But that did not mean that our conversations were easy ones once marriage became a part of our considerations. There was the issue of names. Bob was ready to become Robert Hedge-Cooper, but that seemed ridiculous to me. He was in his fifties and well established professionally. On top of that, I had changed my name when I divorced, hyphenating my mother's maiden name and my father's surname. Changing a name is hard work when you have multiple holdings, and I had worked at the process for at least two years. I was not anywhere near ready to go back through that ordeal again. Besides, it helped me and everybody else to remember that I was my own person. It was not until after Bob's death that I had a twinge of regret that I had never taken his name, but these moments never lasted long. I was who I was. I liked it that way, and so did Bob.

Having been deeply disillusioned by the failure in my marital past, I could not have been more unsure of marriage. At the same time, I knew that Bob could not continue his work if we were not married. As we backed out of the driveway on the way to our wedding, I said to him, "Please tell me one more time, why are we getting married?" It was an absurd question; I well knew the answer, but I was terrified that marriage might take the magic out of our relationship. I feared that marriage twisted love into something hard and unrecognizable—something routinized. He had indulged me for months as I came up with one scheme after another about how we could marry and then get a divorce somewhere where we were not known so that we could live together but not let ourselves be robbed of the delights that an "illicit" love affair might promise. Perhaps we could travel to some romantic place and come back telling people that we had been married there. We never argued about these things; Bob would just let me toil on with my schemes until I found my own fallacies and ridiculousness. I was petrified that night of our wedding, but Bob had enough optimism for both of us. I loved him; that was not the issue. I just had no faith in the institution of marriage. I felt like it ground people up into unrecognizable pieces—and it will if two people are not committed to each other and to the intrigue of the discovery of the other and the devotion that pulled them together in the first place. But I had a committed partner, and I am so glad that I married him. My life might have shriveled up if I had let my apprehensions stop me. Fear is more destructive than anything I know—that and deceptions, which all of my schemes had been.

I considered our relationship to be a very lopsided one, but Bob seemed never to have noticed it. He was a man with five advanced degrees. When he read his Bible, it was in Greek and Hebrew. He could spell almost any word because he had learned well his Latin. He knew the romance languages; he taught himself Italian when he wanted to read Dante in its native tongue (though, to be exact, it was written in a dialect of Italian). He studied Danish when he read and published works regarding Søren Kierkegaard. His interests were wide and deep, and he could speak of them easily. When he delivered talks in Spanish-speaking countries, he spoke in Spanish, though admitting that after days of that, he was exhausted. He had the complete works of Freud in English but wanted them in German. When he last fell ill, he was teaching himself Dutch so that he could read about the Flemish artists in the language in which they had first been noted. Over thirty-four years, our conversations roamed about from one thing to another. He was writing for theological journals, and I for psychological ones, and part of the fun was finding attributed quotations of each other in our writings.

He was formidable; that was apparent, though Lyman Reed said that those who tended to run the other way had failed to look behind the curtain of Oz. One former student of Bob's, Steve Gruman, wrote something to be read at the roast. In it he tells of his first encounter with Bob, saying that he was "quite tall with a strong build. His hair was longish for a professor. He looked like a prophet who had stepped directly from the Hebrew Testament despite being dressed in jeans and western boots. His arms were long and his shirtsleeves unbuttoned."[20]

At other schools, Bob had been addressed as Father Cooper, but on the campus in Texas, it is less formal, so students referred to him as Bob, or Coop, or Cooper. I am not sure how he was addressed by those who knew him less well; it was likely Professor or Dr. Cooper, and there was an occasional Father. He would have preferred that we take no notes in his classes. He just wanted us to bring our brains and, should we write anything down, that it be our own thoughts that had been triggered by his remarks or the remarks made by our fellow class members. I took notes anyway, trying to chisel toeholds in a sheer wall against the blast of ideas that was coming at me, first from one direction and then the other. The name of the author of assigned papers was not to appear anywhere other than on the back of the last page, so that Bob could read without bias. Years later, after we were married, I stood in the balcony doorway, watching him sitting out there reading. To me, he looked magnificent, working away with a toothpick in his mouth (the pipe was gone some time now after a Leukoplakia appeared on his soft pallet). He was barefooted with one ankle balanced over the opposite knee. A soft breeze would ruffle the papers now and then. When he glanced up and smiled at seeing me standing there, leaning against the doorjamb, I asked if he could actually read without recognizing the voice of the writer, "Not always," he said, looking a little sheepish. I did not ask if my voice had been among those he recognized, but after all those conversations, it would be hard to believe that my choice of words and ideas would have not given me away.

Here I, a former student cum wife, stood in the doorway looking at my former professor cum beloved as he worked. But, despite all this discrepancy between our levels of experience and education, Bob could see no distinction in the difference between our levels of power or intelligence. He had always expressed admiration for my mind and the way I saw things. He said that it was because I could instinctively come to truths that he would have struggled with for years. He regularly sought my insight into things. I have no reason not to think that he believed these things to be true; I never felt that he was being condescending toward me, never once. It was not unusual for us to have conversations about the topics that he would be writing about before his work began. "What is psyche?" he would say. Or "What is the relevance of imagination and one's spiritual life?"

Early on when I was one of his students, one of my ways of keeping him in his intellectual cage was that I had given him nicknames. He would know he had a new one when a name tag appeared in his box with the name on it. The early ones were Professor Shit, Dr. Dictionary, and such. Later on, Bear, Frog, Captain Excess, and Bobby were the monikers that only I used; for these there were no name tags. As a child, Bob had been called Sammy or Sam. It had started out as a joke because his father was also a Robert, called Bob, and two seemed too many in one household. To this day, his brother, Gary, and boyhood friends call him Sam, and his nieces and nephews refer to him as Uncle Sam. My niece and great-nephews call him Uncle Bob. In high school, he was called Robert, and from that came Rob. In college, he began introducing himself as Bob. Goodness! How does one keep track of who he is in all that swirl of names? But he seemed to love it when I began adding more and more. When he was dying, our priest and dean of the cathedral, Chris Keller, asked Bob what God called him, and Bob said, "Sam." I bless Chris for that; nothing is more intimate than one's name before God, and if Chris, The Very Rev. Dr. Christoph Keller, III (now there is a name for you), had not asked that question, I would never have known who Bob was when he knelt before God. Samuel, "one called by God" in Hebrew, or "a prophet to his people," was the name he was given—even if indirectly. What had begun as a joke was, in the end, the truest name of them all. I weep in gratitude for that bit of knowledge, that little piece of gold that Chris unearthed for me that day. Later when Bob's journals were found, I read of his own discovery of, and new appreciation for, his name, Samuel. Bob was not always comfortable with his calling. There were times of great doubt. His connection between his earliest name and his calling had come during one of those bouts of doubt in the mid-seventies. And so, he had pressed on. His doubts about himself are so very odd given who he was and is to so many, but we are all allowed, even brought to greater growth, in those times of the dark night of the soul. Someone once said to me, or I read it, that as the hand held close to the eyes blocks all view, so can the immediacy of the Divine leave us standing in the dark. That bit of wisdom was given to me in my early adulthood, and I have thought of it often. One of my professors told me of a Buddhist temple where the statue of the Buddha was so large that one could only squeeze along the walls, seeing only a bit of the Buddha at a time. I have thought about that a long time too. And I wonder, can the fish see the sea when it is ubiquitous? I doubt it.

Laying on of Hands

Shekinah:
the weight
of the glory
of Yahweh
on Israel.

Moses sees the hindparts
of God's glory
as he passes
him, rock, hidden,
bidden to bear
the grumbling squally sack of Hebrews,

I was ready
for most of that
but not for brute
gross flesh-weight
of all those hands
laid on my head

When God shifted
his bag of worlds
to ease his
walking
cosmos-wide; some
old-new part now
is mine—less heavy
though than
green cross-wood.

I bend,
Praise Him!
(Cooper)[21]

Given all of this intelligence, power of spirit, and influence over those whose lives Bob touched, one can easily see why I, who had been told all her life that she was pretty but not very smart, was stunned when Bob said that I was very bright. He had said that I knew the Hebrew Testament far better than he, and I was quick in our conversations; but while I had graduated with honors from high school, done well in college, and had continued to do well in seminary, it never sank in. Just recently, I came across a paper I wrote for one of his classes. There on the back, I read his comments, and it brought back the thrill at the pleasure he took in my work and by his words of encouragement. But early training is of great power in our lives, and if anyone ever spoke the word dyslexia in those days, I don't recall it. Yes, I made good grades, but no one knew how many hours I spent working for them. I often felt dumb.

It was one day when we were having one of our Friday lunches at our favorite Italian restaurant that I heard myself say to Bob something I had never uttered to a soul because I felt embarrassed by it—I wanted a PhD. I can remember the professor of art history who first planted in me this yearning. I admired that man and would have liked to be like him. Upon hearing my comment, Bob set down his fork and with a look of incredulity on his face said, "Well, why don't you get one?" I told him I didn't think I was smart enough. He said very firmly, "Darlin', you are struggling with a poverty of desire." That sentence has echoed through me all these years—and not just about education. I hear it anytime I find myself strung between what I can and cannot do on some old line of doubt. He was so right, and I hear his voice still. It was a poverty of desire that had held me back much of my life, it was a poverty of desire that had made me fear a new marriage, and it was that same poverty that exposed itself that day over a plate of fettuccine carbonara.

I finished my doctorate with the highest possible scores, but I went through with a cohort of people I admired, so I figured we all did the same. It was not until Bob started calling me Doc that it finally worked its way into me. I had actually accomplished something academically that I could place value on. Once again, Bob had given me to myself, and he has never stopped even since his death. Over the years, I heard him say privately and publicly that I did the same for him—that I handed him back to himself better than he had been before. I would hear him say in sermons and lectures that he had learned that to be loved well is to be given to oneself with a clarity and appreciation that one was incapable of achieving alone. We taught each other that there were wonderful things about ourselves to which we had been oblivious. He taught me that I had a good brain, and I showed him that he was not alone in his interests, that there were others who were interested in the things he cared about. His passions were not a burden to me; he was a joy to be with even in the ordinariness of life. He needed never feel alone. As Bob has said about these very things, "love finds loveliness and love makes things lovely."* It was in that spirit that he gave to me a card in which he had written, "You do make bright the world around you. I saw early on that you are epiphany and there's been no reason to change my view. How could I when you are seeing itself? Thanks for being my friend, lover, wife, teacher, guide—I love you, Bear"**

Our conversations could wander wherever we wanted them to go or where they seemed to take us. I was ready to learn from him, and he was just as ready to learn from me. His knowledge was deep enough that I was still learning from him to the end. It is so hard to comprehend, even now. I roll it over and over again in my mind. Watching the clouding over of his intellect was the most painful part of it all. He had given birth to my intellect, and here I was helping him lay his to rest. How odd—how horribly odd.

He had warned me that he was hard to live with. That was absurd. I knew it when he said it. There might be an initial hesitation, but rarely was he in no mood for doing something that I thought would be fun; he would almost always give it a decent try. I can think of an exception, however; he was hesitant, and he was right to be, because it ended up being, for us, a thoroughgoing disaster. Ben and Mary Griffith invited us to join them and meet a group of people for a Labor Day picnic on a hot, humid, sandy, mosquito-populated island off the Florida coast. It was an awful day, but where I tended to try to make the best of things, Bob just snorted around like a caged animal. He completely came undone when it was suggested that this half-dressed, sweat-soaked, insect-bitten troupe play charades. He stalked off to the bathhouse, took a walk, and came back in better spirits. (I wished I'd gone with him; charades is not my favorite thing to do either.) The whole day was so miserable, hot and humid, that years later we were still laughing anytime either of us spoke the words, "De Soto Park."

After the crowd of to-us-strangers left and we were alone with Ben and Mary, Bob eased up. I have photos of Mary, Ben, Bob, and me in swimsuits, wading in the water and looking like we are having a pretty good time after all. It is a measure of their friendship that Ben and Mary continue to be dear friends to this day. Their friendship is an important one. It seems as

---

* In a sermon preached at St. John's Church, Clearwater, Florida. May 5, 1990, on the sixth Sunday after Easter.

** Another note gathered from the kitchen counter.

though no Florida weekend passed that we did not have at least one meal together. Bob and I either attended or gave a dinner party on Friday and Saturday nights, but Sunday evenings almost invariably began with Ben and Mary at our condo. We strolled past the marina where the pulleys and clips were swinging against the rigging and masts, making the sweet sound of a thousand windchimes. To our right were the park and bandstand where no music could be made that was more lilting than that of the sailboats in the wind and roll of the water. Past there, we walked a block or two to one of the many little restaurants in revived downtown Dunedin.

There were many important couples during those years. Ernest and Joanie were among them, of course. Ernest and Bob were the aging remnant of that group of young clergymen who had taken the Diocese of Southern Louisiana by storm during the sixties. Everybody else had either died or been consecrated bishop, which, I think they might say, is about the same thing. Ernest and Joanie would visit us, or we would go to Midland where they had settled. We also traveled well together. No Dungeness crab was ever safe from the four of us, especially when they emerged around San Francisco. Sometimes we would have a reason for going out there, such as a conference, but mostly we were headed for those crabs. One of the craziest things we ever did was drive up one evening from San Francisco to Petaluma so that those two men could dine on duck at a particular restaurant that Ernest knew about. New Orleans was another favorite destination. We were fortunate in our friends and in good times with them.

Before Ernest died, Bob went to spend some time with him, and the two piled up in Ernest's hospital room with a gallon of ice cream apiece and talked about the good times—those long past and those not so far away. At Ernest's funeral, Bob made no attempt to offer a customary homily; he said that no life could be summed up in words. Instead he gave us a medley of poetry and song that did exactly what Bob had said could not be done. He captured the essence of Ernest in his complexities—complexities, the thing that the two men held most in common, that and intellects and a curiosity about the Divine that ranged wider than that of most.

So, for the most part, life with Bob was easy and fun, despite his warnings to the contrary. Even when he fell ill and, in the early stages, could fall into an instant rage, moments of happiness could still find their way through until, ultimately toward the end, when he had forgotten all that annoyed him and all those against whom he nursed old angers; there was nothing but sweetness left. It would now be his gentle soul that led the way. His only concern was that those of us he was leaving behind would all be well. The last words he ever spoke to me were simple words of love, said in that deep, husky voice of lovemaking. To know that you are still desired, what could be greater or more life-giving? It was Bob continuing to give life to me even to the end. I may not have known it always and with any clarity, but that is what I have desired more than anything in life. I was given a soul mate, and death cannot bring that to an end; in some ways it creates a river of love that flows deeper and wider than ever before. His constant words of encouragement and admiration still flow through my mind and heart. It is harder now without his physical presence, but the spiritual connection is increasingly strong. I have had to let go of much, yes, but not love. Love goes on and on and will never end. "Set me as a seal upon thine heart, love is as strong as death ..." (Song of Solomon 8:6 King James Version).

The year after Bob's death, I was, once again, trying to sort through all the things that Bob had packed away over the years. In the correspondence of 1994, I found two letters in particular that brought the heart of him back to life for me in a lovely way. One was the set of notes of a letter that Bob had written to the Rt. Rev. William Spofford and Polly Spofford on June 7, 1994.

> Life is good. I have a demanding, honest and difficult job which I do reasonably well. Ann has interesting and difficult and rewarding work as a psycho-social oncology counselor at the major hospital in these parts, and is working on a Ph.D. in clinical psychology. We live in a beautiful place, enjoy some dear friends, ... take delight in each other's company, and play as much as we can. The most important thing I know about myself is that I am loved.

The second set of notes for a letter are undated and written by Bob to O. C. Edwards.

> I find that I enjoy my work, and know that I have done basically what I want to do in life and I relish what the

> future may hold. It is VERY clear to me now that I want Ann to do and have what she wants, and that I am putting myself second to that. It is a marvel—it is grace—to be married to the most interesting person I know.

Bob and I had to face some truly hard times, but what greater goodness could one ask for than to be loved by the one whom you love and to be found interesting by the one who interests you. I cannot imagine anything more satisfying. Ultimately, and despite all the indignities that he would have to face, my fears about the loss of magic were unfounded. There were some terrible missteps along the way, but to the end, the light danced in our eyes.

I wish I had thought to ask him to write a poem about DeSoto Park. It would have been so funny.

CHAPTER 10

The Rings

... the synchronicity of my desire and my will move together like a wheel. Love who moves the sun and the other stars.

—Dante, *Paradiso*[*]

Over the years, Bob gave me so many rings that I have lost count. The first, of course, was my wonderful wedding band, unless we count the ring that his mother gave him to give to me as an engagement ring. Mabel Cooper was the epitome of a southern lady. I wondered how she would feel about having a new daughter-in-law, but as it turned out, my apprehension was absurd. When we arrived, she came out to meet us. She was dressed impeccably and wearing yellow espadrilles. She greeted me with arms opened wide. I was delighted by her reception of me. She noticed that I did not have an engagement ring, and this did not suit her idea of "proper." Having an engagement ring had never occurred to me, and once we found my wedding ring, I doubt it occurred to Bob. I didn't want an engagement ring. I was slipping up on this marriage carefully. But had Mable Cooper known what was in my head, or rather the absence of what was in my head about an engagement ring, she would not have approved. Instead she went upstairs and upon returning gave Bob a ring that has the wonderful three

---

*

diamond filigree style so popular in the early part of the twentieth century. Bob, realizing what was up and knowing her disapproval of his "oversight," slipped the ring on my finger, and we were official. All this occurred as the three of us stood in the den of his boyhood home. I am so glad that he did not get down on his knee. I could not have stood it. But his mother could breathe freely again. Nothing improper please; let's keep to the conventional! The next morning at the Methodist church, I was introduced to her friends without having them glance down at an empty left hand and then up again at a couple who was traveling cross-country together. The ring was slightly large, even on my right hand, so I've worn it only rarely and then with ring guards and considerable anxiety. I placed great value on that ring. It was the signet of my acceptance into the Cooper family by its matriarch, and while I might not take their name, I did want to be a part of them.

As a means of trying to trick myself into not feeling or looking too married, my wedding ring is not a wedding ring at all. Bob's ring is unusual too. I doubt either one met Mabel Cooper's standards, but she was kind in that southern formal way. Bob was fascinated by the southwest, so our gifted friend, Charla, sketched three potential designs for him to choose among. It was Charla and her husband, Harry, who had taken me in when I left my home and before I had a job and an apartment. It would also be their home where our wedding took place.

I could not decide which design to choose; I was stumped. I called Bob, who was waiting for me at home, and asked him if he would please come choose the one he wanted. He refused—said he didn't want to lay eyes on it until I put it on his finger. Well, that was that! So I, who hates to make decisions, decided which ring he would wear on his hand for very nearly the rest of his life. It was of hammered gold and had four long, thin slices of stones set into it. Three of these were of lapis lazuli, and the fourth, fit in between two of the lapis, was turquoise. That was the perfect ring for the Jung lover who found interest in the idea that three and then a slightly variant fourth represented wholeness. As he grew more ill, Bob's fingers became thinner, and the ring was slipping off into his bed. I found it and returned it to his finger time and again, until one day he spoke the obvious. "It is going to get lost." I slipped it from his finger with sadness, kissed the place where it had rested, and put the ring away. I had dreaded this moment and even talked of it with my daughter Bess, during our previous visit. I sat on her and Kirby's balcony, staring out at the range of Rockies across the valley where the Colorado runs toward the Pacific, and wondered out loud how I could ever find the courage to take Bob's ring from his finger. That is often the way it is with dementia; the horrible future unwinds so slowly, so very slowly before you, that foreboding becomes a persistent companion. But the dreaded moment had now come and gone, and while it was so terribly sad, it was a relief to have it behind us.

Two other rings stand out in my mind. The first was a luscious diamond and sapphire that I saw while dawdling around waiting for a watch battery to be replaced. When I got home, I told Bob about this beautiful ring and how I admired it. I thought nothing of mentioning it, and when Bob said he had some errands to run, I thought nothing of that either. Within the hour, he had returned with the ring in its pretty little box and glee in his eyes. He said he hadn't asked the clerk about the ring but rather about the redhead who had been in earlier. That was my darlin', my dear Bobby—giver of gifts, so many gifts.

The last ring of all came as a pair on the celebration of our twenty-fifth wedding anniversary—our silver anniversary. He was still able at that time to participate in considering what our choice might be, although he did not focus on things very long and only one thing at a time. What we both did know, however—dementia or not—was that the last thing we needed was more silver. We already had mine, ours, his mother's, my mother's, my grandmother's, and even a few pieces of my great-grandmother's. I didn't even want to think about it. I was already up to my elbows in Wright's silver polish and Pacific cloth. Then the idea of rings came up when I saw them advertised. We loved Shakespeare. Bob had studied it, and I had been brought up on Shakespeare, fairy tales, the Prayer Book, and Lily Pons. The idea that we might have found rings with a line from *The Tempest* pleased us both. The inscription reads, "Hear my soul speak." Could the whole quotation be inscribed here, it would say, "Hear my soul speak. The very instant that I saw you did my heart fly to your service and there resides." We were headed now into a time when speech would become more and more difficult for Bob to formulate and to understand (though we never got there). We were going to have to find another way to communicate, and our souls would have to speak for us. That, in the early days, was one of the ways I knew something was going wrong with Bob; he had lost his sense of me on an intuitive level. He was no longer beginning my sentences for me. But by some mystical renewal, we were going to have to find our way back to that and then dig deeper. In our earlier days, Bob composed these lines: "There are places of such silence / in our souls sometimes / though they talk they do not speak"[22] The places of silence were those we were going to have to find.

While he was living, I wore my ring so that the words faced Bob when he looked at my hand—not that he would necessarily read them; it was purely symbolic. When he did have trouble speaking and was getting so frustrated, I would place my hand in his, point to the ring, and assure him that we could figure it out if we relaxed. And usually I was right. His needs were few; he was hungry or in pain or needing reassurance that I loved him and would stay with him. Now that he has gone, I have turned my ring about so that it is I who am reminded that his words and love come to me through his soul to mine. Words of love—always of love. No reproach, no guilt, no sense of things left undone or unsaid—just love, just crystal-like love. Love that seems even now to grow and encourage me toward the future, a love that never ever holds me back but promises me with its every rainbow that the storm has passed.

CHAPTER 11

The Fireworks

Listening to Bob Cooper lecture was
like trying to take notes at a fireworks display

—The Very Rev. Bruce McMillan

It couldn't have happened if Bob and I had planned it, but everywhere we lived, we were blessed with a view of fireworks on special occasions. When he was teaching at the Texas seminary, we lived on the side of a rather steep hill that fell off quickly down toward a creek before the land spread out toward the river just beyond. To give us even more of a lift, our condo was three stories high. We had moved in on the last day of June, gotten settled on the first of July, and then married that evening.

Though our wedding was quite small, we were inundated by flowers and greetings sent by kind and understanding friends who were not among the invited. The condo looked like an English garden. And we delighted in it. Bob's bishop in California telegraphed the blessing to be read at the conclusion of the service. He had seen what was coming between Bob and Bishop Benitez, so he had taken Bob aside at some meeting and suggested that Bob transfer his canonical residency from Texas to the diocese in California. In reality, this move may just have angered the fellow in Texas all the more. As a consequence, he could not get around to giving permission to any of the priests under his charge to perform our marriage. So our dear friend and Presbyterian minister, Ilene Dunn, did it using our cherished Book of Common Prayer. There were so many clergy at our wedding that it was hard to find work for everyone. Will Spong was both preacher and best man, Bill Green celebrated the Eucharist, Charlie Cook read the Gospel, and Bill Adams read the blessing from the telegram that the bishop had sent. I am sure I am leaving someone out; time has eroded my memory. Lynn Schaefer was maid of honor, and all my friends helped make the whole thing come off smoothly. I sent Bob to pick up a round of cheese that I had ordered, and he decided we needed two. Do you have any idea how long it takes two people to eat or give away twenty pounds of cheese? That may have been when I dubbed him Captain Excess, but I'm not sure; there were plenty of occasions on which to have done so. As Bob would say, "Mercy!" Fortunately, Charla and Charlotte handled the rest of the ordering and picking up, and someone other than I did the setting up of chairs and the tidying up afterward. Harry would have had a big part in all of that, and Lynn too.

I found myself surrounded by family that night. And after the service, Rebecca hugged Bob and called him "Daddy Bob," never knowing that was what Bob's father had been called. It brought tears to Bob's eyes. My children became Bob's children; he loved them as one would love his own. We never pretended that they didn't have a father in their lives, but who has so much love that they can't stand more? We had just returned from seeing Bob's mother and brothers and all the extended Cooper family. But I am sure Bob would have liked to have had them there too. I was so pleased to see Bob welcomed into mine so warmly. And Rebecca's gift of his special name stuck. To this day, when we reminisce, Rebecca and her children call him by that name. Bess, who is more reserved and never presumptuous, called him Bob; that too was fine by him.

Will was never known for his sartorial genius, unless we are talking in terms of the *genus insaniam*. He appeared that night dressed in a shirt with broad black and white stripes; he looked more like a referee than a best man. Well, Bob and I had always said to each other, after one of our tussles over one unimportant thing or another, "We are too wise to woo in peace." That is a rough recitation from Shakespeare's *Much Ado about Nothing*. I don't know who said it. I think it was Benedict to Beatrice, but it certainly applied to us. But the point is that having someone around as referee might not have been such a bad idea.

It was a lovely evening, as was the next morning with my family. It is only after the flight to California that things begin to blur for me. We took a thousand photographs, but they are all so amateurish. As a consequence, there are not all that many wedding pictures in the scrapbook. We might not have had any of the family brunch if the camera had not been passed around. I love all those people, and so few remain; time has marched them off the stage. Bob, Will, and Bill Green are gone. All of them had been my professors. Lynn, my maid of honor, is gone—died so young. Dorothy Dacy has left us. Papa died years ago. And of those of us who remain—we scattered like hammered mercury.

That morning following our wedding, my family joined us for brunch and a visit. That was the second of July. On the third, there was a party, and the Fourth of July was dedicated to recovery from all this activity and to packing for our trip to California. We had been caught off guard by the fireworks. We were in the uppermost bedroom when suddenly the reverberations and flashes caught our attention. What a wonderful surprise; we had not even considered this when we bought the place. The following day, we flew out to the Bay Area and that evening had dinner with a group of friends who lived there. I recall being with Joye and Bill Pregnall and Mark Linenthal and his wife, Frances Jaffer. Fatigue was beginning to catch up with me. The next day, we drove up to Ernest's coast house at Point Reyes, where I collapsed and slept for twelve hours straight through. I woke up to Bob, who was a bit anxious that I was not well.

After the rush of getting married, our wedding trip was a very quiet one. It had been our habit to make forays inland to the wine country, but I don't recall that we did it this time except once when we drove back toward Petaluma for dinner. It is frustrating now, but I don't remember much of that wedding trip other than trying to recuperate from the mad whirl of moving, marrying, celebrating, and traveling; the memory of it has blended in with other trips to the same area.

Another thing I recall about that trip was that Mark said at dinner that he had found, while living on the East Coast, that his life was more about time, but on the West, it had become more about space. That has stuck with me over the years. I don't necessarily want to live in Southern California, as beautiful as it is; I would miss the seasons there just as I did in Florida. I do recall that when I was doing my doctoral work in Santa Barbara, I was dreamier and more disconnected there than ever. Once a month, I would fly out after work on a Thursday afternoon and attend classes all weekend. Then on Sunday, I would fly the red-eye back into the time-maddened East Coast, where life was very different. I was also working in a hospital setting where time was of the essence. I don't think that "spacy" is quite what Mark meant by space, but I was caught up in the mesmerizing quality of California, its dramatic beauty and the vastness of the ocean, and that understanding might make less hash of what Mark was trying to convey.

As I have grown older, or perhaps because of Bob's passing, I have found in myself the inclination to live in a more evanescent way. Perhaps it is a consciousness of time that exhausts itself as we age; it passes by so rapidly and quietly. I have the sense that I am just floating through this world, that I am passing through as time has become less and less relevant. I like life much better this way; I am more at peace.

Carpinteria, the little town outside Santa Barbara where I stayed on those long weekends and the longer summer quarter, is among the most charming places I have lived. I look back on it now and wonder where the energy to do this traveling, working, studying, and loving came from. Bob often spent time there with me, and the place became a part of him as well. When graduation time came and we were leaving, I asked Bob to write a poem for me; we would be rolling back eastward like the rush of the waters created by the rising of the great mountains. This is what he wrote:

Pangaea

"... 225-million years ago ... most of the Earth's land was linked
together in a vast, single supercontinent called PANGAEA."

There wasn't always a California
Even though we believed all that we've been told
That it rose up from the semen foam sea
Like Aphrodite from the genitals
Severed and cast there in mythic revolt
Later we believed that the great river rose

In Texas and ran for millennia
A quarter billion years to Nevada
Where the coast dropped off into ocean
Nobody saw this it was before
There were gods goddesses or even names
We're still looking toward where we came from
And cannot even say the words dumb blind
Names do not come into our mouths until
Millions of years are gone it's Pangaea
We say everything was earth unbroken
But the sea the sea was there forever
It left its traces we're told that this is so
That the Venus of Willendorf fractured
Herself her breasts here massive are mountains
Her *mons* is the cleft of canyon and draw
The oldest woman yields the oldest places
The world is a woman's body her parts
Make us we have come to this peaceful place
To find the names of what never was once
Gods goddesses souls myths the four winds follow
Converge on this fragile shore we're awake
Hear our own words tumbling out of our mouths
It's California it's Pangaea
(Cooper)[23]

Not long after returning from our honeymoon, it was time to begin wrapping up the work in my studio and preparing for our trip to Boston for Bob's sabbatical. When it was done, the real fireworks began and not always the lovely celebratory ones. Bam! All kinds of grief came loose to harm us all as Bob and Benitez squared off. When the dust settled, Bob and I were headed for Florida with a considerable jingle in our pockets and a heaviness in our hearts. It was not the easiest of moves, and as a consequence of my having injured my back, a forlorn Bob got into my car and drove to Florida alone, where he rented a suite in a hotel on Clearwater Beach, one that had a beautiful view of the Gulf. It was there that we stayed until more permanent lodgings were found. Only days after I arrived, I would have my first back surgery. Afterward, I would lie awake at night and be fascinated by the thunderstorms way out over the Gulf. Tea and other simple things could be prepared in the kitchen. A wonderful deli was nearby on the island. Best of all was a goodhearted housekeeper who tended to me, looking in on me several times a day. Will sent some flowers, and that spurred me to find my watercolors and begin painting. It is not the best work I have ever done, but it hangs in the hallway now as a reminder of a dark time that opened onto the most blissful time of my life.

On one of our preliminary trips to Florida, we were house hunting and saw a building that was on a promontory with an incredibly beautiful view of the intercoastal. Our Realtor had said it was not the place for us to live. But it stayed on our minds, and when we asked our new friends, Mary and Ben, about it, they assured us it was a lovely place. Mary, who was also a Realtor, made the arrangements, finding a view from the seventh floor with a southern exposure and water views from every room. When the movers arrived, I was still near helpless following surgery. As Ben and Mary unpacked my kitchen, I lay there on the living room floor, bewildered. I was not at all sure of anything. With me still struggling to get through my day, Bob was having a hard time too—blaming himself for the total upheaval in our lives. One day, he took me to lunch. I always wanted to go, but then I would get out and be in so much misery that I could not enjoy myself. On this particular day, I was seated on the world's hardest chair and hurting terribly. I looked at Bob so forlorn as he sat there across the table. I thought to myself that I just couldn't stand being an emotional, physical, and every other kind of burden to him any longer. I made up my mind that I was going to like being where I was. It was sheer will. Deciding to ignore the pain shooting up my spine, I said, "You know, Bobby, I like it here." I saw him beaming; his lines of concern collapsed into that exquisite smile for the first time since he had met me on my arrival. His face just fractured from a grim look of concern and stress to that wonderful smile. What fascinated me all the more was that I felt better, immediately, and from that time forward, I did like the place—a lot.

Once again, New Year's Eve brought fireworks right smack in front of us. Anytime the fireworks came, our living room would be filled with folks. Elsa and Rick Nail, Steve and Donna Clark, Sally Foote, Dick and Sue Cobbs, as well as the Griffiths and Bob's brother, Gary, who had now joined our cluster of friends. So far, all our new friends were members of Ascension parish where Bob was functioning as a member of the staff. Despite this common connection, we had all met in various ways. To that were added Frank King, Meta and Carl Gustafson, and Don Stein. We were blessed with so many others as the years went by.

When the festive nights arrived, barges loaded with pyrotechnics were launched into the intercoastal channel, and the show began. Fireworks are great, but fireworks on the water are even better. These were wonderful evenings. At Christmas, we also enjoyed the water parades. Everyone who had the desire and a boat would string it up with lights and make their way up and down the canal.

We moved into our Little Rock home on our wedding anniversary in 1997. The heat and humidity had been so terrible that the workmen walked off the job at noon, leaving the drivers to do the job alone. To make matters even worse, we live on a hill so steep that the truck had to be parked on the lower street at the side of our house, and furniture was pushed up the hill on hand trollies or loaded into Bob's truck and driven up. John Blackwood, my brother-in-law (I always want to say my "brother" because that is the way I think of him), came to the rescue. For the first time, Bob had become very disoriented; he just wandered about. All morning, the simpleminded movers kept asking him where to put things, and he, every time, would refer them to me. They never learned. That just made him more anxious. He and I had sat in bed for weeks before with little rooms drawn to scale and paper furniture that I had cut out. Carefully we had decided where each piece would go and glued it into place. He had been excited and clear as a bell, but the drive to Little Rock had exhausted him, and he was just lost. He could not seem to remember that each room had the little map of the furniture labeled and taped to the doorjamb. It was not a good day. And when we got things in place and the hubbub had stopped a couple of days later, Bob was back to himself again.

As is predictable, the heat brought rain and then a cool front that cleared it all out. That Fourth of July was the coolest I have ever known in southern climes. It was a beautiful day. When the sun went down, we were astonished to discover that the country club across the valley from our house had an elaborate and lengthy display of fireworks. We could not believe our luck! It was now three for three—three homes and three surprising firework displays. There were evenings at our club thirty floors up over Little Rock where we saw plenty of fireworks at Christmas and on Memorial Day; these were wonderful but not like those evenings in our home.

Then one of the sweetest evenings of all came when we were staying at El Teatro, a lovely boutique hotel in downtown Denver. Our vacations now involved finding elegant hotels and spending our time there luxuriating in our rooms. Bob was not well enough to do much more than that, and while neither of us said anything, we knew this most likely would be our last trip out to Colorado and possibly the end to vacations altogether. The last evening there, we had gone down to an elaborate dinner with wine pairings. As we started back up to our room, we were commenting on how it could not have been a more perfect evening. Our room was graced with enormous windows, and the west ones looked out on the Rockies. We stood there holding each other as the last rays of light lit up the thunderheads over the mountains. Then out of the blue, the southern windows fired up. Fireworks! Lots and lots. These were being shot off for some celebration on a rooftop just below and across the street from us. We had a grand view; it was almost as if we were inside the explosions. We could not believe our good fortune. The next morning, we bundled up precious-dog-Charlie with his bed and began the drive toward home.

Should I ever move again, and I pray I won't, I do not expect that I will continue to have fireworks in my view; that was something sparked between the two of us. But I bet I will at least glance out the window come the Fourth of July and think about times past and the surprise and excitement of those days when the skies blazed.

CHAPTER 12

The Frog

He offered then to mentor me
As poet prince, no longer frog -
And I of course said 'yes' and more
That day beneath the woodland floor.

—Linda Ori, *!The Frog Prince*[24]

Bob was delighted by crystal; well, *we* were delighted by crystal. One weekend, we had made a trip to Houston and wandered into Gump's to see what they had. We found some lovely delicate wine goblets that I had been yearning for and made our way home with six of them. But what Bob had spied and wanted was some Baccarat. He had especially hankered for a pattern called "Nancy." It was lovely (it was Baccarat, after all), but it was all straight lines, not the soft, curved lines that I preferred. However, I was so pleased by this man who loved lovely things and charmed by Bob's enthusiasm that it was easy to keep my mouth shut. I thought it would be a nice thing to give him for special occasions, but Bob was buying it up so fast I didn't have the chance. The pieces began rolling in, especially after our move to Florida, where he had a ready supply at Bailey Banks and Biddle. With all the barware collected, he turned to vases. I use these larger ones with trepidation. They are quite heavy, and without strong arms here to heave them about, they tend to stay in the china cabinet. We usually shopped together, or I tagged along might be more accurate. If I was away at school, I could be sure that a pretty piece would be waiting for me on the kitchen counter when I returned.

When the family would ask what Bob wanted for Christmas or a birthday, I would tell them Baccarat, but they never took me seriously. I suspected they were letting themselves slide into the conclusion that only women like such things—that I was just trying to feather my already overly feathered nest. But it made no difference; they wouldn't have had a chance. I think the last pieces were bought after our arrival in Little Rock, and the penultimate (one of Bob's favorite words) was a beautiful, clear Christmas tree, and the last of all was a lovely red puffed heart that he gave me as a Valentine. These latter two stay packed away in their boxes and come out for their special occasions. There is something about the heft of them in my hands that makes them among the holy objects that are now mine. Seeing them brings to mind the pleasure he received watching me discover what gift he had for me this time. After the fussing around of decorating for these special days, the tree or the Valentine were the last things opened and set in place. There was great delight in doing this when Bob was in my sight; and now that he is away, there is delight mixed with sweet sadness that comes from an enduring gratitude that the Divine was so good to us and that the best of all gifts was the gift of one for the other, even now that he is no longer within my reach.

There is another Valentine, but I don't try to touch it anymore because it has served its purpose and has no more to say to me. But the memory of it causes me to get chills. It was in the weeks after Bob's death when I was struggling with taxes and the probate of Bob's will. Many of the same papers were pertinent to both endeavors. I was not well and anxious about a surgery that was leaving me with little time to get all odds and ends wrapped up. I had spent an entire day going back and forth through the same stack of papers, trying to find things that I absolutely knew were there because I had already seen them there two, sometimes three times, on that very day. It was now dark outside, and I was beyond exhaustion. I needed to give it up for that day and come back when I was rested and fresh—though, in truth, sleep was not to be had by me of late. Finally, feeling completely defeated by my inadequacies, I gathered up the papers and started for the closet where I could put the documents out of sight. I could not quite realize that this house now contained me and no other; my desktop would have been as good a place as any other to leave them. But as I reached for the doorknob to the closet, I heard, coming out from under my chin, the tune that had the words "I love you just the way you are." I could not have needed that invasion of mercy more than I did in that moment of defeat. I flew back to my desk and began going back through those papers one more time. There from out of them came a big red Valentine, the last one Bob had given me just weeks before. He had sent one of his aids, Joyce, to buy it. I pounded on that button time and again; it had sung its last. But I got it—I got the message. I was doing the best I could, blinded as I was by grief, the absence of sleep, an inability to eat, and simply a fear of what might happen next. My grief was so crippling that the failure to awake from surgery would have been a welcomed relief. But I did not want to leave things in a mess. I was putting so much pressure on myself to get all things in order.

The card was there the next morning, just as red and big and sweet, but silent, except in my heart where it sang. I was still adored just as I was, and that would prove to be adequate if I would be gentle with myself. What only I could know was that Bob had said similar words to me in the darkest days of my life, when Bishop Benitez held me hostage for the choices of another. Bob would say, "I will take you any way I find you." Now he had spoken again, and I, feeling more capable now, got the important things done based on Bob's confidence coming from beyond. Now, three years later, I am trying to get everything done. My funeral is planned, all the financial matters are in place. But the attic, that damn attic, is an unending nemesis for me. You love me, Bob Cooper; so please tell me why you had to keep so much stuff, and why is it up there where it is so hard for me to get to? And why should a princess be encumbered with so much work and so many decisions to make?

One night not long after our marriage, we were having a small dinner party. Bob was in his funny mode, and the people we had invited were bright and witty too. We were carrying on and having a hilarious time making as much noise as the garage band next door. At some point, I apparently said something imperious. With perfect timing, Bob turned to those assembled and said, "You know, I married into East Texas royalty." Well that nearly put an end to the evening because we all laughed ourselves silly. So "Princess" it was from that time forward. I did tell Bob though, in a quiet moment—I wouldn't want to have embarrassed him—that I thought he would have to be Frog. No matter how many times I kissed him, I saw no signs of transformation. He just wasn't prince material. He latched on to that, and from then on, his name for himself was Frog. Frog was hopping off to the office, or Frog was hopping to the grocery store, or Frog was hopping to have his ears lowered (a Cooperism for haircut). Wherever Frog went, he hopped. I would have preferred that he be Bear; I called him that often and had given him every bear fetish I could get my hands on as we traveled the Southwest. He enjoyed the bears, but he still called himself Frog. If he was speaking of himself as a child, he talked of the polliwog. I had created a monster.

While I was giving him bears, he was finding frogs. Two came from the Jackalope in Albuquerque. One was huge with wings, and Bob attached it to the ceiling in his library. When we shifted his library from that room to a larger one, the frog stayed where it was, now presiding over the guests who stay here. It is funny how one just stops seeing things, and that is the way it has been with the flying frog. As I wrote this, I stopped to go looking for it, and there it was where Bob had hung it when we moved into this house more than twenty years ago. He took pride in this house and told me on the day we moved in that the only way he would leave here was in a box. He said it was the most beautiful house he had ever lived in and he never wanted to move again.

There were other frogs. One winds up and comes hopping at you. Out on the terrace, there is a pair of bronze dancing frogs that we bought at the Serendipity in Dunedin, Florida. They are facing each other, holding both hands, mouths wide open with laughter as if they are whirling in a circle as kids do. There is also the slinky bronze frog who sits on the edge of the bookcase, looking at us in a sultry way as she leans back on her hands, ankles crossed. And there is the frog gazing ball that was given to him for his birthday; this frog looked much like a fat Buddha until a terrible spring storm put him on an extreme weight loss program. Bob kept him because he never threw anything away, and I still have him because he makes a good hiding place for the key to the terrace gate.

But years after all the frog stuff got started, I found *it*! Baccarat made a frog with a little golden crown tilted on its head! I have never been so excited to find a gift for Bob in all my life, and there had been jillions of them by this time. So proudly the frog sits with all Bob's barware, where he prefers to nestle among the champagne flutes. I never see him that I don't think of shopping sprees and laughter and the hopping frog. How beautiful, how precious, how lovely were those days. And how sublime it is to recall them. I sure miss Ol' Frog now that he has hopped beyond my sight. He didn't take his crown with him; he must have been confident he would be issued another one on arrival.

CHAPTER 13

The Dictionaries

... But for death
I cannot complete
What I thought
I knew
How to begin

... But for Death
—Robert Cooper[25]

Bob was a lover of words, a wordsmith. He is the only person I have ever seen who literally read dictionaries. I have given away so many among his collection, and there are still shelves more. Most are English, but other languages are there as well; and I should not forget the dictionaries of street slang filled with profanities and the laughter with which they were read. Along with all this fascination with words, Bob had a one-man mission of preventing the corruption of the English language, while at the same time messing around with it. If things were to be *shared,* they were to be torn in half and a piece given away, not some bit of information told to one person by another. That was telling someone something, not sharing. Sex was a word for gender, not for an act. And *quality?* It was neutral; the question was whether something was of good or bad quality. The list of misused words that aggravated him was nearly without end.

The same was true of misconceptions; the idea of casual sex or free love, as it has been called, could send him into a rigor. In his opinion, these were oxymorons. Love cost something, there was nothing free about it, and there was nothing casual about sexual acts because these too were costing somebody something, not to mention the sacred element invested in them. When Bob was a young chaplain at LSU, Bishop Nolan called him to his office. The opening salvo was this: "Father, what's this about your advocating free love?"

Bob replied, "Well, sir, I don't believe there is such a thing as free love, so I can hardly advocate it." The bishop was clearly relieved. It seems that some unfortunate co-ed had her pills discovered by her daddy, and she said the first thing that came to her mind—that Fr. Cooper had said it was all right. Consequently, a phone call had been made by an irate father to the bishop, and the call after that from the bishop to Bob. I don't know how the story ended, but I am glad that I was not the bishop. We know what can await the messenger who reports unfortunate information to someone who is already irate.

Bob always claimed, and I never doubted it, that one of his favorite academic efforts was a paper that he presented before an august group of scholars. I have not yet found the paper, which he claimed was well received. The subject was the etymology of the word fuck. Its seems that there is quite an argument about its origins—Old English, Germanic, Dutch, and Norwegian. Bob's claim that it is a word that began with somewhat credible sources and was based on legal documents recorded as early as the twenty-third dynasty in Egypt. If I am figuring it correctly, and that is quite an if, that would have been between seven and eight hundred years BCE. I'll just leave it at that, and anyone who is interested can track that piece down; it would be worth the effort. The word had been outlawed in England and the US in the late 1800s, and this attributed to it much power—a greater power than it ever had before. But it was always clear that for Bob it was not so much a power word as it was one of those workable words and a perfectly accurate substitute for the misused word sex. He did not use intercourse; he would say, "Why use a polysyllabic word with various meanings when a simple word would do?" I have heard him use copulate when the explicit was more than the sensibilities of his listeners could bear. In his opinion, lovemaking was not a bad thing to say, but he considered it a euphemism that did not carry with it the clarity that he preferred in communication. So, if this boy from North Carolina wanted to talk about sexual intercourse, he tended to talk about fucking or teased his audience with "sexual congress" (always getting a laugh with its archness). He said this with an uppity accent that he often affected when he was encountering the absurd. And what was the absurd? An example of that would be an audience that was using the so-called slang at every turn in their daily lives but thought they had to clean it up for a seminary campus or at the men's retreat or because Father was present. At the same time as all of this was going on, he did not offend the sensibilities of those who simply would have found in its use confusion or, worse, aversion. Most of all, he had been brought up to be a polite southern boy, not just an academic nincompoop. Accuracy was to give way to kindness. And what would Mabel Cooper have made of this? She would have been mortified by the whole thing, and I am sure that her early training served as a considerable governor over what he would have said and where.

He did not frequently use it as profanity, but instead he tended to use it judiciously in conversation and seminary lectures. If one heard it from him, it was usually in a proper sentence with a subject and a predicate—sometimes as a noun, sometimes as a verb, or gerund—just a regular word without a lot of silly energy around it. However, it was another thing when it came to shooting the finger. If I wanted to do it, it would take both hands, and, even then, there would not be much elevation to the finger of import—so why try? Not with Bob! He could fold down the three and the other shot to the stars. He used this arrangement of fingers to direct traffic.

But shit was another thing. If he made a mistake or had a close call in traffic, he could spit that out with such rapidity that it could almost sound like a striking snake. But if he was simply disgusted or if he was fooling around with friends, he said it as if it were constructed of many syllables. This was his language along with a vocabulary that was astounding. The whole time he was ill, there were vocabulary and grammar lessons for those of us caring for him. The last week of his life on this earth, he used a word I had never heard before. It has slipped from my memory now, but when I looked it up at the time, I found it to be a rarely used but proper word that hung close to its Latin etymology. His knowledge of words was so vast that he still knew far more than I on the day he died.

When he first arrived on a seminary campus to teach, he must have come as a shock. His first call was to a place that practiced a particular kind of piety that gave it a kind of formality that could never be found on secular campuses where Bob had previously taught. Clergy and students were expected to conduct themselves in particular ways both in and out of chapel. But what are you going to do with an extraordinary professor who simply cannot find it in himself to follow along with the minutiae of daily clerical life? Much of the time he couldn't even bring himself to dress in a clerical collar. He wore sandals until the winters got so cold there were no options. It is said that on one occasion when the then archbishop of Canterbury, Michael Ramsey, was visiting the seminary, he asked Bob where his shoes were, to which Bob replied in a respectful way, "Your Grace, when have you ever seen Jesus in shoes?" I might also say as an aside that Bob was very fond of this man, perhaps even devoted to him, and I gather Bob provoked a hearty laugh.

Students, who were taught earlier on than I, tell me that he was teaching one day when a sincere young seminary student was appalled by the North Carolinian when the salty language began pouring forth. After class, this student had the integrity to come forward and say how offended he had been by what had just occurred. To this, it is said that Bob replied, "Don't blame me; blame God. God is the one who sent you here. I didn't. I'm just the appointed affliction." That was the wit and speed of thought that either made you laugh or sent you away with your head shaking. He had been causing trouble in school since he was in kindergarten. I've got the report cards to prove it.

It seemed that Bob was his own man; over the years that I was in school, he often said to me, "I am free." I heard it often enough that with time I came to wonder if this was just whistling in the dark. I never heard him say it again when his straining for perfection had largely passed. I do not know what that meant or if it meant anything at all. Had he lost freedom or found it? Or had he realized that it had never been true? I would have had it that it was always true, just that it no longer needed to be said. I found him wonderful just as he was, and I hope that that was even more liberating for him. It was not until he was ill that I found myself feeling protective of him and guarded about how he was being perceived by others. It was so hard to surrender to the inevitableness of the disorder and to let him be as he was without searching for the smoke and mirrors that would make things seem other than they were to outsiders. That was not the case when we were alone. I could still enjoy him, pajama clad as he was. And while he was a different man, he was always a surprisingly amazing one, who continued to have a startling intellect to the end—despite the odds he labored under and despite the major reduction of his cognitive capacity.* Somewhere up out of the fog came these remarkably lucid times. But he was no longer that tall, straight, brilliant man whom men and women sought out for company. No longer did everybody want a piece of him. But I did—just as he was.

* I want to remind my reader, especially those tending to someone with dementia, that Bob died of other causes before the horror of end-stage dementia overtook him. His abilities, though frightfully diminished, still remained.

CHAPTER 14

The Sad Little Clock

Memory Saint Augustine has taught us
Is visceral the mind's own craw its belly
Or it is he said sometimes where we regress
And strangle in their bed the sequelae
Of our lost past

—Robert Cooper, "Looms of Our Mother"[26]

Before we left Florida, I had become concerned that something was awry. Bob often seemed depressed and irritable. He was having a hard time concentrating. One morning, he became enraged when there was no hot water; in actuality, he had gotten the taps confused. My hope was that it was the pressure of a stressful and difficult job, funding a nonprofit while at the same time carrying a full patient load. His blood pressure was swinging wildly. I began to press for him to give up this position and find one with less stress. It was a hard thing to ask because we had such wonderful friends in the area and had been a part of the social scene, which both of us enjoyed. But where were we to go? Bob was now sixty-two, and the job market is not inviting for a fellow of that age. Then he was offered a part-time job at the cathedral in Little Rock. We came to visit, fell in love with the cathedral, the beauty of the area, and the support of the arts that we found in the city. Arkansas would be a place where we would have good health care available, and the cost of living was relatively low. We found a beautiful house that weekend. The best part was that we would be near my sister and brother-in-law. Ever since Bob's brother had moved from Florida, there had been a sense of lack. It would be nice to have family nearby again. The move would mean that Bob would have to take early retirement, which would reduce my benefits should he go before I, but I was not concerned so much about money as about Bob's health.

But the miracle I had hoped for with the relief of Bob's stress never came. Stress had not been the villain all along, as I had hoped it had been. Bob was better but still not himself. The blood pressure remained just as erratic, and the curious calcium levels continued, and heaven knows his agitation continued, an agitation that I believe now to be the consequence of confusion and its disorientation. He no longer knew more than anybody else in the room. Then he could make an immediate switch and be himself again—loving, kind, considerate and brilliant.

That year was the year I defended my dissertation. We returned home from Santa Barbara and right into a steady rain that went on for thirty dark, chilly days, during which I had a terrible cold. I began studying for my licensing exam. I turned myself almost inside out over that thing. I was going to open a private practice. We joined the ballet society and flirted with the symphony guild. Bob became a docent at the Arkansas Art Center. I joined a study group of psychologists who met weekly at the med school. But I could not get Bob to do anything that would make it possible for him to resume his practice. We had always worked well together, and he could have joined my practice with ease, I thought. But he would not even renew his memberships in prestigious organizations where he was a diplomate. It was so unlike him. We tried to teach a class together, and it was a disaster, we both agreed on that. Coteaching was something that we had found enormous pleasure in for years before. He was still doing some writing, and most of this was published, but when he received a rejection of his theory of an Odysseus complex, he quit writing too. As I was going up, he was heading down. We were completely out of sync. I was totally disoriented by this, and I suppose he was too.

Finally, he seemed to get some footing when he began studying art history at the University of Arkansas, Little Rock. He would not, however, enroll as a student in classes or work toward a degree. There was no reason for him to do that, but this was a man who had collected degrees for years, one after another. This was new behavior; the very ambitious, competitive man was not ambitious at all. Not many people take time to write a note after a death, though there is nothing more comforting; however, one of the letters I received was from a man who had been an art professor of Bob's at UALR. In that note, he told me what a pleasure it was to have had time in Bob's company.

I kept nagging Bob's physician to focus on the calcium counts. These erratic counts had been going on for some time, long before we left Florida. I would go to appointments with Bob or write letters for Bob to take. I think that the conclusion was more that I was a nut than that the counts needed closer monitoring. Bob's memory was being affected by something, even if I was the only one who was taking note. He never learned how to use the thermostat on our heating and cooling system. He couldn't seem to remember in which drawers the silverware was kept. The way he parked his truck in the garage was becoming an issue between us. Finally, some more thorough and sophisticated testing was done; the results were helpful. Bob was referred to an endocrinologist, and then to a surgeon who removed a tumor from the parathyroid that was one thousand times the normal size of the gland. Bob's brain had been sloshing in calcium that had been leached from his bones. Poor man, he had been very sick and basically neglected by one physician after another for seven years. Within hours, Bob was Bob again. There had been some damage in the brain cells; the truck would continue being parked in the middle of the garage. Permanent damage had been done in the part of the brain where spatial matters are assessed. But we could live with that if I had my happy Bob back, and he was still strong as an ox. We did quite well for a while.

One day he was headed for a regular checkup. We were standing in front of the French doors, my head on his chest as we said goodbye; that's when I heard an irregular heartbeat. I asked Bob if he wanted me to go with him. It was going to take me a few minutes to change clothes. No, he was going to go alone, but he assured me he would ask for particular attention. It was atrial fibrillation. There would be one thing after another as we aged, but it was all surmountable until the botched hip replacement, followed by a fierce infection at the surgical sight. Six weeks later, when he got home from the hospital, it was clear that he was not himself. His short-term memory was markedly changed. The trauma of the previous weeks had exposed my terrifying suspicions of earlier years. I was back to suspecting that dementia was an underlying problem. Bob was depressed and disagreeable and in terrible pain, pain that never ended, salved only by death. I thought it was just me with whom he was out of sorts. I walked on eggshells. Then I began to realize that irritability was far from limited to me. Once again, I couldn't get the doctors to pay me any attention at all. Bob would tell them that I was a hysteric and then strike up a conversation about Aristotle or art and its nexus with medicine, and they would think that no brain like that could be a sick one. He may have been losing his short-term memory, but he was clever nonetheless. Time was wasting; I wanted him on some medication to slow down the dementia, if that was what it was. Finally the doctor relented and ordered some diagnostic exams.

To my surprise, Bob did not resist the idea of a neuropsychologist. He got out the map, found the office where the testing was to take place, and drove himself to his appointment. That is not the behavior of someone with such a severe disorder, but Bob's baseline was so high to begin with that he had plenty of brainpower held in reserve. For that reason, I wondered what the results of the testing would show. I was in my office when the neuropsychologist telephoned. The phone rang while I was with a patient, so a message was left for me to return the call. Dreading what it would be, I braced myself against bad news. I took the phone out on the back steps of the building before I punched in the numbers. It was as if the enormity of what I was about to hear was too great for the space in my office, and I needed all the air I could get.

This was the moment I had dreaded for years. I had always known that because of the differences in our ages, I would likely take care of Bob when he was older. Dementia was my greatest fear, and now, like Job, my greatest fear had come upon me. The examiner began by saying that she had not yet informed Bob but that as soon as we hung up, she would call him to make an appointment for the two of us to come in. She would go over the results with us then. She said something about professional courtesy and then proceeded to tell me what I already knew: he was failing. Dementia would take his brain bit by bit until Bob would no longer be Bob. It seemed to have begun in the frontal lobes, and this explained the drastic change in his personality, the petulance and empathic failures that those of us close to him had struggled with. This was at the root of his near loss of metaphor, the cause of his tending to take things so literally. I wondered how it could be possible to hear a diagnosis like this about oneself, learn of the bleak future ahead, and still be able to endure. But endure he did; he was stoic.

I kept my focus on the papers set in front of us. He was scoring very well on large portions of the test, but he had drawn his clock with the numbers outside the circle, a marked demonstration of a brain that is not processing or perceiving properly and a common difficulty of dementia patients. Time was distorted. Time was melting away and taking memory and Bobby with it. This sad little clock had been drawn by the man I cherished; it was not some illustration in a textbook. And I was looking at it as a brokenhearted wife, not a professional.

At the same time that I was feeling devastated, there was also a sense of relief that, though it was about the worst that life could throw our way, it was not just my beloved being hateful or trying to drive me away. Now I could understand why he would no sooner have a tantrum and say cruel things to me than he would be telling me he loved me with all his being. Before the diagnosis I had been totally bewildered and beginning to doubt my own sanity at continuing to expose myself to mistreatment. But the test results showed something different. He was not angry; he was in trouble, and the trouble was organic. Somewhere, beyond illness, his soul still loved and cared for me, and yes it was troubled by what had been happening to him. One afternoon after one of these episodes, he said to me, "My soul is sick." But once the diagnosis was made, Bob seemed to relax into it and stop fighting against it, and consequently against me and anyone else who crossed his path. He made certain that his affairs were in order. He had already turned over finances to me some time before because it had become so aggravating for him and he had made some costly mistakes. He was still driving though. It was time for him to give that up.

My daughter, Rebecca, had begun making the habit of visiting us monthly. She and Bob loved each other and had since early on. Daddy Bob had been there for her in some of her dark times. The three of us were sitting at breakfast one morning. I was headed for my office, but they were free to go have some fun. For lunch, Bob suggested that they head out to their favorite hole-in-the-wall for oysters and anything else fried that he could get his hands on. I, who had refused to be his passenger for a long time, said to him, "Please let Rebecca drive." He of course was offended and began to mount a defense. Rebecca, sitting to his right, simply and sweetly reached over and lightly laid her hand on his arm, "Daddy Bob, when you drive, I feel frightened." He looked shaken and then, taking a deep breath, told her he wanted her to feel safe, took the keys from his pocket, handed them to her, and never drove again.

There were some terrible times when he felt he could not go on, but these were fleeting. Such grace! I would see that same grace in him time and time again. In the end, I knew him to be even more amazing than I had ever before known him to be. I stand in awe of him today and pray to be as accepting in facing my own end as he was in facing his. The greatest gift of all was that his passing came long before he was completely undone. He continued to know us. He still had a sense of humor, though it was not as esoteric as before. It would be hard to overstate the strength of character and surety with which he met his end.

There is a prayer in the Book of Common Prayer that Bob had prayed over my father's open grave, and that Bob and I had prayed together in the evenings. "O Lord, support us all the day long until the shadows lengthen and evening comes and the busy world is hushed, and the fever of life is over and our work is done. Then in thy mercy grant us a safe lodging and a holy rest and peace at the last" (p. 833 BCP).

At every point, Bob was able to give bits of himself away with serenity just as he had surrendered the car keys. I believe that despite all these losses, at the end Bob knew peace. And that is mercy. That is not dementia. The prayer that Bob prayed more often than any other all his adult life was that God would have mercy upon him. How often had I heard him say it, and how often it appears in his journals. I hope that I was a part of that mercy. I know that the people who came to help us were. And his presence in my life was a great mercy. Now I must live without his tender touch. Have mercy, oh God, have mercy.

CHAPTER 15

The Letters

Letters mine and others'
Lost small records
The passing of what I am
What I was

—Robert Cooper, "Gone"
(Bob's last attempt at poetry)[27]

With lovers, there are so many dreams—we will go back to France, tour St. Petersburg's Hermitage, return to Tuscany in the fall when the grapes come in, spend more time in Greece so we can wander her hills, and on and on. But no dream is so powerful that it can overcome the certainty that at some time we will have to part. Whether it came with my graduation from seminary or because of the death of one or the other, parting would come. There is something closely linked about love and grief. Now death has come and gone, yet love remains, and grief has come to join it. But love does have its limits. I could not love Bob back into good health, though God knows I tried, and Bob's love for me could not put an end to disease either.

Chris Keller, who knows a great deal about grief and loss himself, said to me not long after Bob's death that grief is "the other side of love," as he put it. He went on to say that where there is love, grief will be a part of it. I heard him and knew that what he said was true, but it hit me with a terrible thud, as if I had never considered it before. For if this link were so, and I knew it was, I was bound to grieve forever. That conversation took place over the phone, but I am sure it was clear to Chris that I was shaken by the truth of what he was saying. I was still in that raw stage of grief and desperate for it to pass. I was waiting both unkindly toward and impatiently with myself. I wanted to get "beyond grief"; the pain was so acute. I believed there was something profoundly wrong with me. Chris was telling me in his low-key way that there is no such thing as getting beyond grief. The curious thing is that accepting the reality of his words made my days easier to endure. I was now less likely to wake in the morning and regret that I was alive. I struggle often, but I am finally past that time when I could not imagine a future without Bob's physical presence. I am helped by the sense of his spirit, the promise of my deliverance from this world, and the belief that I will again be united with him. St. Augustine wrote, "*pondus meum amor meus,*" in *Confessions,*" my weight is my love." I have considered this for a long time but especially since Bob's passing. Perhaps Augustine was saying that he was held in place by love or perhaps that he was in bondage to that which he loved. I've never been clear exactly what he had in mind. But for me, love and its companion, grief, are that weight as well as that bond. I am bound to Bob, and that love holds me in place, but not in the sense of being held fast to one place. I am bound to be with him as he goes forward. And the most astonishing thing for me has been the realization that in longing for Bob, I have learned what it is to long for God.

Victor Frankl said that suffering ceases to be suffering when it finds meaning; Carl Jung said basically the same thing. That day on the phone, Chris helped me to find meaning in what was threatening to become a crippling grief. Buddha said that in the end what mattered is how we loved, how gently we lived, and how we let go of things not meant for us. Bob's physical presence was no longer meant for me, and I had to let go. I've come some distance with that latter, but I still have a long, long way to go. Perhaps this is a task without end. I long for his touch. I think that I always knew, despite my fears of failing him by departing this earth first, I would be the one lingering behind, yearning. As time went by and his health grew more and more precarious and his memory increasingly fragile, I sometimes thought that I was like Jackie Kennedy crawling out onto the back of a speeding limousine, trying to gather up the bits and pieces of a life that could never be put together again. Along with all the wonderful things that love brings, it also brings with it the hurts and sorrows of the one afflicted by illness and grief to the one who seems to be remaining intact physically. Bob wanted me to reassure him that I would always be his companion along the way, and I pray that I am.

In thinking again of how Bob was fond of saying that he believed in three things—bodies, wonder, and grace—I wonder more and more how he had the grace to resolutely hold on to his physicality as he withered.* He loved his body. I don't mean that he admired it, though no doubt a kid who took seriously weight lifting, basketball, and survival swimming knew that he was blessed with a strong, healthy body. And the fact that he had something sarcastic to say about every young male who had long hair gave some clear indication of how much he would have liked to have had more of his than he had. But what I mean by all this is that he loved the pleasure his body gave him. Sexual pleasure was very high on that list, as were good food, drink, and a luxurious environment. I, who had always made ends meet by scrimping on groceries, came face-to-face with a beef-devouring, caviar-savoring whisky drinker. He enjoyed pretty things and once told me that of all the sins, his greatest was the lust of the eyes. Through all the years we were together, he would walk into a room and say to me, "We live in a beautiful place." Paradoxically, despite all this talk of bodies and things, he was not a particularly materialistic man. In earlier days when he was in his one-window loft, he loved the Spartan "monkishness" of the place. He had his books, the rocker that his mother had rocked him in, a broken lamp, and a sleeping bag. It was a good secluded spot for him to sort out the scramble of his life.

Desert

(It matters whether)
The earth throws itself at the sky here
or the sky casts itself onto the earth
like a cloak with holes of fire in it

* When Bob said he believed in bodies, wonder, and grace, he was not limiting himself to the body made of flesh; he had a great interest in the body of the resurrection and would return to the theme often in sermons, essays, and in speculative conversations that the two of us had over the years and in the months before his death.

(better cold than burning)
leaving itself naked and burning

or is it both

for at the horizon who can tell who leapt first?

Were I shorn of all I've loved of people
I would find the now nameless desert place
the Trappist kind of place and live undone
but for watching in the summer sky at dawn
Aldebaran Rigel Sirius
The heliacal rising of the stars
and settle who started all of this
whether earth climbs or sky falls
the answered query worth the years
the shuddered prayers of every still every moving second
(Cooper)[28]

When we were closing the Cooper home after Mabel Cooper's death, I came across a packet of letters Bob wrote to his mother during his travels in the summer of 1956. I pitched them in a box with other odds and ends. Bob showed no interest in them but had never thrown them away either. On a cold, rainy afternoon after Bob's death, I was sorting through his things and came across the letters again. This time I had the leisure to read them. Most had been written from Edinburgh while he had been studying there. This was the summer of 1957, and it formed a lifelong reservoir of growth and insight for him.

Bob came back to the United States (the "Untied" States as he would have said) and finished his degree here. By this time, he had expressed a desire to go into the priesthood. His letters written during his first semester in New Haven are filled with the delights of scholasticism. He took classes at both Berkley Divinity School and Yale. He toyed with the idea of seeking an additional degree in art history but settled on taking some courses instead. (While he was doing this, I was a kid in high school. But when I got to college, I majored in art and art history.) He graduated magna cum laude and was assigned his first church, or rather two small churches, in North Carolina. With the exception of his troubles in the mid-sixties, his journals seem to show that he was reasonably content most of the time; like many of us, he went through cycles of discontent—some more severe than others. Life moved along like this until the turmoil when he was fifty. Having eventually made his way through all this, Bob wrote his mentor and friend, Winston King, these sad words: "I have divorced. That has been, I believe, the saddest and at the same time the most hopeful thing in my adult life. Nothing really prepares us for such things. I regret the hurt and harm that I have surely done for years, but feel very alive and hopeful."

Divorce

How can I tell him
that he cannot leave her
She is flesh of your flesh I'll say
She is bone of your bone
You knew each other so long
from boyhood from girlhood
You will ache for her
with the hollow hurt
bit into the fruit of Eden
the mouthful that can never be
put back right
when you've once chewed it
I will say to him
that like a land hoed and plowed
that has learned the set of your foot to the furrow
tasted your singular salt
she will not release you
I will speak to him
of their children
standing now
like three unequally aged trees
separating the properties
of old and angered friends

I will inquire of him
how they will be divided
to what sawmill be sent
how be given again to the earth
from which they sprang
But if he demands of me
a less quaint idiom a less bucolic speech
I shall ask him
with what fiery scalpel
he will sever gene from gene
in the chemistry of paradise
with what grinding calculator he will
unscramble the chromosomal algebra
get back again what is his
give back again what is hers*
(Cooper)[29]

I also found, in the box of letters, a very skimpy white swimsuit that I had also gathered up years before. It had been standard issue for the survival swimming courses at Georgia Tech. That was something he had pulled out of the carton when we returned from closing his family home. I laugh now as I recall how he put it on to admire himself in front of the cheval mirror in our Florida bedroom. It is amazing that he could get into it, but then his friends in high school hadn't called him "Hatchet Ass" for no good reason. There he was in that suit, and I would swear that the fellow who looked back at him from the mirror was nineteen years old—and had all his hair. What did remain unchanged from those swimming days was a beautiful, long stroke; it seemed that he could make the length of that Olympic pool in one smooth glide. I could have watched him swim forever as I sat there under my umbrella. Those were sweet days.

There were masses of letters still in Bob's files, and there is a box full of letters that I wrote to Bob when he was traveling. The latter were written to be read at various hours of each day while he was away from me. I wrote letters, and Bob wrote poems. Rebecca has sworn to me that she will destroy my letters at my death. These were only intended for Bob's

* I found this scribbled on scraps of paper from a Nashville lumberyard.

eyes—and how he had loved them! Many are letters tucked inside funny greeting cards that I found along the way. Before these particular letters were ever thought of, Bob and I had exchanged notes while he was away on sabbatical and I was doing my clinical work in Houston—he the professor and I the student. This communication is innocent, kind, circumspect, and of a sort that, in hindsight, reveals two people who were doing their best to express the importance of the friendship without going over the edge. He had told me about the acceptance of his Kierkegaard manuscript and quoted the complimentary words of the editors, "... you have surpassed yourself." My reader can imagine how bittersweet it was to find that actual letter with those very words. Tidying up behind a lost loved one can be a thing of many emotions.

While my letters of those years were read only by Bob, Bob would eventually submit the poems for publication. Upon hearing the following poem, a friend asked me what it was like to have one's love life published for all to see. Often I was unaware of the upcoming publication of these love poems until Bob presented them to me in their published form, and on one occasion, I had been seated in the audience and introduced as his muse before he read a series of them. But in the instance of the following poem, he had asked me to do an illustration of a panther to appear with the poem. It was not used daily like Annie and Princess were, but Panther was one of his names for me and the one earliest given. When he used it, I knew we were moving into his deep, inner world, and I loved it as I loved "instinct itself" (Cooper). So how did I feel about the poems being published? Loved.

The Panther

It wasn't merely woman that brought you such a distance
for whatever it is lies lower down is singular
in *one* woman that she who'll stay the night with you plants
in you in your humus the lure and the smell of her lair

It is animal darkness and the moist heat the damp glance
in the eyes their two bright slits burn and whose body is fair
promise that one mile more two at the most opens on the dance
on the frenzy and the limbs of Dionysos your share

> In the dun tangled low copse of hair at the bellies' bourn
> first things and last the secret place where you and she are born
> (Cooper)[30]

I read these poems with enormous gratitude and marvel that I was the focus of such a profound love by a man who was not afraid of his emotions or of giving expression to them. He poured his heart out to me in every conceivable way. In the beginning, I had been almost ashamed because I did not know how to love him in that same way, or at least I didn't think I did, but with time I relaxed into it. The ability to tend to him in the end was an opportunity to show myself just how much I did love him. He had said early on, "I love you any way I find you." Now it was my turn to show him and myself that I could do the same for him and love him the way I found him.

There are also masses of little notes that Bob placed on my carrel, inviting me to drop by his office. Most of these are drawn like cartoons with little ducks or bears asking the question. On later notes, the frog joined the zoo of his little characters left on our kitchen counter. I always thought that if Bob had ever studied drawing, he would have done well. He had so many gifts that there was not enough time, even in a very long and healthy life, to have pursued all of them.

The shortest of all notes were those written by me on strips of ribbon. They mostly read, "I love you." He never threw a single one away even though I had not realized that and continued adding more and more to his carry-on. Over the years, he had strewn them through hotels, taxis, and airports trip after trip as one after another slipped past the zippers and dangled until it found the floor. I had tucked them into every corner of his luggage, briefcase, and shaving kit. I am quite certain that if I climbed up on the shelf in the laundry room and pulled down his luggage, I would find ribbons. I'll not look; if I found one, I would weep the rest of the day. How fleeting our time together. If I were given the chance, even knowing how painful life can sometimes be, I would live my time with him all over again—every moment of it. Nothing could surpass the goodness and beauty of it. During his last week on earth, Bob said to me, "We had class, didn't we." Yes, darlin', we had class, and love, and delight, and an abundance of goodness; there are times when I find the breadth of our good fortune hard to believe.

A friend said to me one day that he knew that people admired me for the sacrifices I made for Bob and that he admired me for that as well. Then he said, "But do you realize what Bob sacrificed for you?" This man did not know Bob; they had never met, and he had never seen him or read any of his work. But intuitively he knew what I knew. Through his illness, Bob had shown me, once again, that I was capable of more than I had ever thought myself capable. He also showed me what faith was. Oh, yes, he had his dark moments, but he always found the light again. How could faith come to be faith without sorrow? Once again, as he had done so many times before, Bob gave birth to me. No doubt that continues to go on today. When someone has given their life for you, you can never be the same again.

Grief never goes away, we just learn to do it better.

—Anonymous

CHAPTER 16

The Cassock

[She] reaches to pull
her cloak about her
the piles of memories solid
solid as he about her again

—Robert Cooper, "About Her Again"[31]

I don't have any idea where they came from or how they were acquired, but there were two of them—the cassocks, that is. Mother was the one who had gotten them. Someone must have traveled to Rome and brought them back. Her intention was to use them as costumes for two of the three kings in our Christmas pageants at St. Matthew's. The cassocks buttoned down the front and had a cape attached around the shoulders, called a soutane. Both were piped in cardinal red and made of heavy black wool. They had been made for a man who must have been quite slight because they fit my young, thin, but fairly tall frame without dragging on the ground by too terribly much. I loved wearing one. I don't remember any made-up games around them (we had gotten a little to grown-uppity for that, my sister and I). Nor do I ever remember wanting to be a priest—an acolyte yes, but not a priest. That would have been beyond my imagination. I just put one on and traipsed around in it throughout a winter's day; I liked the feel of it. But that cassock rode too easily on my shoulders not to have had some profound effect on me in some bodily way. In those days, the only women who stepped beyond the altar rail were members of the altar guild who performed their services in empty, quiet churches; their ecclesiastical garb included white cotton gloves and a Kleenex bobby-pinned to the tops of their heads to satisfy St. Paul's admonition that women were not to offend the angels by exposing their hair. (Those angels must be in a mighty state of vexation nowadays.)

In time, I would expose myself to much pain and disappointment before I was definitely and finally persuaded that my calling was to minister outside the church—and in many cases, to those horribly wounded by the church. I have not turned my back on things ecclesiastical. I would and do teach there again, and I find great joy in working with the cathedral's flower guild (sans Kleenex). There is something about working in a quiet and deserted church; the holiness of the space has always been intriguing to me. And in this case, it means that I am working at altars where Bob once stood and celebrated the Mass. I did not join the guild until after his death, and I do not know, even remotely know, how to describe the physical sensation I experienced the first time I stood behind the great altar and looked out into the cathedral as he had done so many times before me. I do know that I briefly wondered if I were going to faint. That sensation was gone as fast as it came. And it wasn't exactly fainting because that is a loss of strength, and this was more like a force that was overwhelming to me.

For almost 150 years, people have come to this site to celebrate or grieve or simply to pray quietly for guidance or for the desires of their hearts. There is something about the accumulation of all that spiritual energy that creates some swirl of a Divine force that people like me insist is there. I feel every emotion that can be felt when I am bathed in that pool. The human and the Divine flowing together brings tears of hope to me or perhaps just sheer joy that wells up from the holiness of the place. Bob would have said of that day when I was standing there behind the altar that God had surprised me with joy; he was insistent that God, as joy, comes always as surprise. Whatever it is, I feel overtaken by it there in that place. When it comes to the teachings of the church, I have strayed somewhat from orthodoxy, but you will find me there most Sundays because there is something for me that I can find nowhere else—some archetypal structure that speaks to my soul, something that heals me, sets me upright when I am down. There were a few years that I did not function at all in the church, and I was persuaded that that was because God had called me out. For a time, this cradle Episcopalian attended an African American church, and those people were so good to me. Bob never pressured me at all, *not at all,* during this time. Finally, toward the very end of his illness, I was reeled back in again by the kindness that Chris showed Bob in his final months. The funeral cinched it. I was back home. When I returned, there was a difference. I was clear that the church was a gathering of God's people, sometimes better than many, but people nonetheless with all the same failures and flaws. God was not the church, and whatever confusions I had had about that, I had shed. My theological shifting could be just that; I did not need the church's stamp of approval to be there in what I experienced as a sacred place. My conscience owed no one anything. I was free. That could not have been said of me a decade earlier. It had been more like an obsession then, that I would show up for services.

I don't just feel connected to Bob there; I do not want to cheapen this by trying to capture it and limit it to my personal experience. Instead, I feel my connection to all who have gone before and those who come now—the communion of saints it has been called. But not just Christians have found their way to this hill; the Quapaw were here long before we showed up, with our modern trappings and convoluted theologies. That brings to mind what Bob would say, "There can be no wall of separation built so high that it reaches to heaven." We are all of one blood and created so by the hand of the Almighty, or by whatever name we choose to give to the Divine. I just stumbled onto this place. It is not mine to possess.

But I began this by talking about cassocks, and Bob has a sweet story of his first encounter with a cassock, and I want the story to be told in his own words. He addresses some of these same issues. This is an excerpt of a note written to the writer of a letter to the editor that had been forwarded to him. It addresses an error of fact that he had made in the biographical statement about a poet. Bob wrote this letter in response, expressing his gratitude for the correction. The writer states that she had "stayed" in the church. Picking up on her word, he writes:

> When I was six years old my two older-than-I girl cousins took me to Lenten school with them at St. Luke's Church in Salisbury, North Carolina (my family were Methodists).

> I went the following Lent with them and still have the silver cross engraved with the dates, 1941, 1942 (my Daddy was in the Army in those days). At that time, as a boy I fell in love with the fabric of the building, the colors, the smells, the sounds and the hushedness of the place, the feel of the dark wood in the darkened nave. Voices were always lowered then in those days in church. I remember looking up at the tall priest to whom my cousins introduced me, and I recall as if it were today the feel of his wool cassock as it brushed against me. I was converted then, at age six. It was a conversion of the body, of the sense, and I still hold that that is the best conversion of all. I would like to believe now that I fell in love with God then by having loved those hearty things ...
>
> When I was a college student my mind was converted, but there was a certain self-consciousness about that, a certain pretension on my part. After all it was the church of W. H. Auden, T. S. Elliot, etc.! My mind has wavered with the changing winds of doctrines and the foibles and frailties of us all many times since then. I have been a priest for nearly thirty-five years now, and I have from time to time had some minor importance in its doings. I have been not only blest by this church, but terribly harmed by it as well. At times I have loathed it, but that hasn't lasted.
>
> Over a long period of fits and starts I have learned (almost) finally that the church and God are not the same thing. Obvious? Trivial? Not for me, it wasn't and isn't. I have been in agony sometimes, but ... I like giving my body and my mind—one thing—up to the flux, flow, and rhythms of the liturgy. This body believes even when I don't.

So with these experiences as a boy and now having become a young man, not yet twenty, Bob had presented himself to the curate, Terry Holmes, who described Bob as breathless, having run all the way across town. With great enthusiasm and in one breath, he blurted out, "I want to be confirmed, and I want to be a priest."

Bob's wool cassock hangs in the closet now, but I know nothing of the little silver crosses. Every time I make the sign of the cross, touching fingers to forehead, to chest, shoulder to shoulder and back again, I remember Bob's words—"sometimes my body believes when my mind will not." There is a certain peace in that—in the realization that all of this is beyond my mind's capacity. John Calvin wrote in his *Institutes* that he experienced more than he understood. I can say the same thing.

It has never occurred to me till now, but Bob's cassock just might feel good and comforting on a cold winter's day like this. It would hang off of me much more than the ones from Rome did when I was a girl. But I think I will put it on and see. I can stop worrying about what I should do with it, stop trying to find someone to whom it could go, and let that answer come to me when it will. Surely somewhere along the way, some tall, broad-shouldered priest in need of it will cross my path. What I shall do now is sooth myself in its capacious folds and rest here by the fire as I remember the priest in western boots who wore it as he made ash crosses on our foreheads and reminded us that nothing mortal lasts forever—neither pain nor gladness. We are all just passing through, and the view is an ever-changing one.

CHAPTER 17

The Walnut Box

I promise you an easy promise
Every face is different is the same
You will find me in a dream
Recumbent as memory is

—Robert Cooper[32]

In Bob's library, there rests a beautiful walnut cigar box that has an inlaid brass plate on the top that is engraved with Bob's initials, RMC. In it are the little bits and pieces of life that meant something to Bob at one time or another. These are a parking permit from the University of Texas where he had enrolled to take an advanced course in Spanish, an ID from the seminary, and two cards from Pan Am that had at some time given him some sort of privilege. These last two are the dendrites of his travels about the Pacific. He had most particularly been in Hong Kong, where he was served the eyes of the fish. He loved things Asian as a probable consequence of his years studying Eastern religions. He has two scrolls that translate, "Coming from a thousand books" and "Sitting in the gateless gate." These still hang on the living room wall.

When I look at these scrolls, I now think of the afternoon that Bob awoke alarmed from an afternoon nap. I heard him rise from bed so I quickly started in his direction. He had dreamed that he and a business partner were constructing an office building but that explosions of dynamite were occurring at the site. He was using his walker but moving so fast that he backed me into a scroll, causing it to make an odd sound. A look of horror came over him. "There it has happened again!" I was trying to calm him and show him that I had made the sound by rattling the heavy paper. I made the mistake of touching the scroll again to show him what I had done, but he held his head in his hands and cried, "Oh dear God, it has happened again." I can promise you that he is somewhere among the heavens laughing as I write this, but no one was laughing that afternoon. It took him a long time to get that all sorted out and to calm down. I felt like a heel, having just made things worse for him. I made him some lavender tea, and he sat in the living room as I made one of my phony calls to the newspaper to learn of explosions in the area. They "reported" to me that there had been none reported but that they would go to the work site near the cathedral and call me if there were problems. Within minutes, when no report was returned, Bob had me call them again. This time they wanted him to know that there had been sounds in the downtown area but that no damage had been reported or found, and there were no injuries reported either. It was just a mystery. He could live with that, so we cuddled up by the fire and drank our tea in peace.

It was Bob's teacher and mentor, Professor Winston King, who had been so important to Bob's study of comparative religions years before. In more recent times, Mrs. King had struggled with dementia. The professor wrote of this with such care and devotion. I was always amazed by his equanimity, and I would go back and reread the letters when I was worn and frayed with concern and care—or in times of outright failure such as this. The professor's letters had trailed off at about the time Bob was diagnosed. He lived to be a very old man but remained vital; what struck me most about him was his capacity for letting life come at him, all the while having, as his central concern, the well-being of his wife. He was physically strained with her care yet remained at peace. At least it seemed that way. He talked of how he was eager to keep the realization from her that she was failing. I read these particular letters again when I found myself facing the same concerns as he. It was as if he had left me a chart through rough waters without realizing what he was doing. After his wife's death, I watched as Professor King's handwriting grew increasingly shaky, and he began to repeat himself, stating that he was uncertain of what he had written before. But his sense of peace never seemed to come to an end. I always supposed that his years of study and his practice of daily meditation were helping to hold him together. I have a monkey brain, and meditation is not something that I have ever done well or for extended periods of time, though God knows I have tried, and with age have improved. I relied on prayer, and I did make time when I could remove myself from the fray and just sit quietly for a while. Gardening was another relief for me; there is something healing about working in the soil.

The presence of these bold Chinese scrolls, into which I had backed, is a bit jarring, hung as they are in a room that is largely seventeenth-century French. I just remind myself that the Chinoiserie was popular during that era in France and move on, leaving them there even though the one who took the greatest delight in them is gone. These are here because Bob was interested in religions. The Gautama Buddha reclines beneath the sofa table, while the fat Buddha sits at the ready by the bar. The gilt Ramayana deer presides over the living room hearth. These are magnificent pieces, and while I was with him, Bob was the real shopper. Sadly, I cannot remember the exact trip when we got the Buddhas. The fat one might have arrived when Bob did. But I do remember with exactitude the day when we were strolling down Royal Street in New Orleans and found the Ramayana. I could almost count our New Orleans trips by the things Bob bought there: the crystal punchbowl that now sits on my desk filled with oranges, or the little silver salt spoons that we bought for our Boston-acquired salt cellars. Bob marveled at how I decorated our homes. He claimed that he had no vision of how things would turn out. But he excelled at finding lovely things to place in it.

But while these things have stirred memories, they do not fit into the walnut box. What is there are two ticket stubs to a performance of Sam Shephard's *Buried Child* that we saw on February 25, 1988. Bob was powerfully affected by the play, and quotations from it turn up in things he wrote and in the sermons he preached. I am sure that his students heard of it too. Because of his passion for the play, I have learned to quote lines from it just by hearing Bob repeat them so often. It has much to do with memory, and it is startling to see just how often Bob wrote in poetry and prose about memory and being remembered. It is a recurring theme in the play, bleak as it is, but it fit right into that preoccupation of Bob's. Toward the end, he could not remember that he had had lunch as he was leaving the table, but his retention of older things amazed us all. As I have said, he took our leave before he forgot us, and that had been my constant prayer, that he go before he was massively undone. I am overwhelmed with gratitude for that. I have fought with God about one thing or another much of my adult life. I have demanded and then sulked when my demands were not met in the precise way I had instructed. But the gift of Bob's deliverance from the hands of dementia has brought me to my knees. I don't think that I can fuss anymore. Not everyone who has asked for mercy in the face of dementia has received it in that particular form, and often mercy goes unrecognized. God knows, it is not earned—at least not in my case. I have often had reason to think of myself as one of God's problem children, and that is why I am so grateful for loving-kindness, the *chesed* of the Divine, wherever I have had the grace to perceive it. And that love was so much easier to experience once I moved away from being a self-righteous prig. It was Bob who was the instrument in pulling me through that knothole. Life is so much freer now, and joy so much more present to my perception.

After Bob's studies at Edinburgh, he went with friends for a trip around England—London, Oxford, and then on to Ireland aboard a wooden ship that made creaking sounds all through the night when all else was quiet and there was nothing to which one could pay attention. He loved telling me about that voyage and wrote for me at least one poem about it. That whole experience of Edinburgh was a revelation for him. On the voyage over, he had met a fellow passenger who was on her way to Paris, where she would continue her doctoral studies at the Sorbonne. He was smitten with her; she, who was a bit older and far more sophisticated, had been a bit on the seductive side. But like most summer romances, little came of it except thrilling memories of her. I think though that this was his first exposure to a female intellectual, and he liked that kind of company. For the rest of his life, these women were among his friends, and it was good for him; it brought him energy. Tucked among his other memorabilia is a sixpence—a memento of that time away from the familiar. It bears the image of the lovely young queen not far from the outset of her reign.

And that brings me to the angel tie tack given by two of our Florida friends. They had asked Bob if he would meet them for breakfast one morning a week to talk about angels; he was happy to do so. One of these women is Elsa Nail, who became a close friend of ours as well as the physical therapist who helped me to walk normally again after my first back surgery. The other is Sally Foote; she, like Elsa, was a member of the same congregation where Bob was serving and I was attending. Sally is an attorney and regular supplier of citrus since our move to Little Rock. Both of these women are great company, and they and Rick Nail (also an attorney), along with us, had considerable interest in fine music. We five would go to the opera house in Sarasota during the season. There were no operatic performances on our side of Tampa Bay, so it was off to either Sarasota or Santa Fe for us. The three angel talkers (though it is reported that their conversations ranged far afield to even deeper and more perplexing things) had a great time over early breakfasts, and on frequent weekend evenings, we would gather at the Nails' house and eat wonderful Italian food with Pavarotti pounding away in the background. Good friends and good times. When Bob was ill, music was on almost all of the time, night and day. Now the house and I sit in silence. I am not exactly sure how it started, but now it is a habit that I have no real urge to break. The music that Bob and I had enjoyed had now taken on my melancholy tone, and green grief had no need of compounding miseries.

When Bob had grown weary of managing a full teaching load, he was also tired of traveling, but he continued into the late eighties for financial reasons. He told me at the time that he had lived hand to mouth all his adult life. More than once he said to me, with regard to the frequent traveling, that he sometimes felt like the mouth that walks. I seriously doubt that those who heard him speak experienced him as such. But toward the end of 1985, he told me that he thought he could stand little more of it. He was booked well into the future, but he planned to stop accepting invitations. Again and again, he expressed how he felt reduced to little but words. To my astonishment, I came across a wind-up toy that is a mouth that snaps and feet that walk. To it, I attached a note that reads, "Traveling Companion and Pinch Hitter for The Mouth that Walks." There in the walnut box is the funny little toy with bow and note intact. I suppose that had been its resting place for thirty years. Once we were able to pool our resources, that angst about finances ceased, and he seemed a different man.

Also in the box are two shells. One is a perfect sand dollar that he picked up one day when we were out on Dunedin Beach. Few people went there, and that was fine with us; the crowds of Clearwater Beach or any of the other barrier islands held no real interest for us. The day Bob spied the sand dollar was a blustery day in what Floridians call winter. One can look a long time before a perfect shell can be found on a rocky beach; consequently, he was so delighted with himself. The child was still alive in him; I saw him at play that day.

The other shell is a tiny little scallop shell. Our move to Florida was hardly a smooth one. One day I was painting a bedroom wall, getting our condo ready for selling. Bob was taking a nap on the sofa in the living room downstairs. If I have a head at all, it is marked by an impenetrable skull. I do not like asking for help. Apparently one of my rules inviolate is that if one person is working, the other does not nap! I bent over and tried to yank our bed from the wall single-handedly. I had had a problematic back for a long time, but that tug did the trick. A disc ruptured. I tried everything to avoid surgery. When it was time to leave for Florida, Bob had to go it alone.

Rebecca and Bess looked after me. "Bec" would stay nights and most of every day doing the painting that I still thought needed doing. Bess handled the business end of things, including the oversight of packing. When it was clear that I was getting worse, not better, I got into a wheelchair and was loaded into a first-class seat, ice packs and all. It was a *pluperfect* mess. When I arrived in Florida, I couldn't walk even a few steps without help. Bob and brother Gary met me at the airport. When Bob bent over to kiss me, he pressed that delicate shell into my hand. Three days later, I was rolled into surgery.

The deal on the Florida condo that we wanted to purchase had fallen through. We were living in accommodations on the beach, so Dick and Sue took us to their home for the first day or two after I was released. Mary took over the search for finding us a permanent place to live, and it did not take her long. When finally settled, we realized that we were in one of the most beautifully situated condos in the country, and the window treatments were already in place. Bob wouldn't have to hang any more curtains—ever.

Praise to the Mole (Homage to Kafka)

Five times he has stood on various things
And hung draperies and curtains in houses
He did not own. Not owning houses brings
To his mind always the mole that drowses,
Subterranean in the long dark sleeves
Of his life. It rouses hope of breaking
Through the surface, for he truly believes
There is a light that is healing, blinding,
That can turn him, nourished, out of himself.
Perhaps inside himself there is a light
To assure him. It would ignore the pelf*
Which he strives so to keep from his sight.
Out through the earth, which is only a skin,
And once its broken through, nothing will cow
His emerging. He will shed the dirt akin
To darkness and resolve things: but for now,
A broken shade, he hangs between two lights.
With hammer and warm nails he pays the toll
That buys him freedom from the outside sights,
Pays it piecemeal to the burrowing mole
(Cooper)[33]

Bob was no handyman anyway; things tended to be a bit askew if he did them. In our Little Rock house, he took it upon himself to hang a little sign on the half-bath door. It is not plumb, and when the time comes that it must come down, I hope someone will think of him who followed a carpenter devotedly but who could not properly strike hammer to nail himself.

Among other things in the box are the little figures that I had made from pipe cleaners. As I go through these things, I realize that the things that I had something to do with were always made or bought to make Bob laugh. I loved his laugh and his smile—two of the greatest things in my life. Another example is that of Vincent van Duck, who has a blue smock, a palette and brush, and a bandage over one ear—should a duck happen to

* Poverty

have an ear to lose. Recently I brought him back down from the attic and placed him on the stool in the library. For years, he was on display in our bedroom wherever we lived, and before that in Bob's office.

At one point, we had given each other so many stuffed animals that we had to make choices. Now all but Vincent live in the attic, and that includes the white bear that is almost as big as I am. I got that on a birthday celebrated in Florida. Bears were numerous among our things. But Vincent van Duck is the most sophisticated of all these creatures. Now with small children in the family again, as the next generation comes along, it is time to bring the critters downstairs again so that they can play. Those at play will not include Vincent—he is far too cranky—and perhaps not the little duck Splendor, sitting in her grass; she is far too delicate. But the giant bear, he loves children.

That sad summer after I was turned away from ordination, Papa took me and Bess along with him and his girlfriend on a cruise in the Caribbean. We put in at the American Virgin Islands, and while there, I bought a box of Jamaican cigars. Aside from the walnut box, two things remain of Bob's cigar days: a cigar band from the cigars of that trip and a three-by-five card from Florida days that has this exchange. First, Ann writes, "Thank you, I smoked it—it was nice." With a response from Bob written below, "Smart Ass!" He had left a cigar on the kitchen counter. I couldn't miss the chance to write the note and drop the cigar into the drawer below. I was gone when he found the note and left me his reply. We had some dark times, but we never quite forgot what it was to be playful and how to do it. The cigar band and the note were in Bob's box of memories when I opened it.

While I was on that cruise, Bob was away on a speaking tour and, on one occasion, sleeping near a Japanese garden that had in it one of those wonderful bamboo waterfalls. He wrote this poem with his trip across the Irish sea in mind.

And Ships, an Ocean

You told me you wrote ever since I spoke
about the wooden ship how it knows its own
sounds its joints creak an old woman at home
easy in the house of her wet bones

I had spoken about the crossings at night
From Glasgow to Belfast on the Irish Sea
(I said you said I want to make love
to you in the water's way of moving)

Now you write that I am the swell over you
that under us everything rides

The running water is all there is

Now I sleep by the Japanese garden
all night I hear it the *tsokubai*
water is flowing along the bamboo sluice
falling on into the small pond
the living sound broken only by mind
into thoughts into words

Bosui told me this

Each voice is a bell
The sea is every sound there is
Your eyes are open
(Cooper)[34]

The next item in the box will be remembered by longtime Episcopalians. It is a pendant with the face of Jesus looking distinctly Western European on one side, and on the reverse side words that read, "I am an Episcopalian." I laughed when I saw that; I would have been an adolescent, but I think that I once had one of those myself. Bob enjoyed telling the story of Will Campbell, the well-known Southern novelist, a Baptist minister, and also the husband of an Episcopalian. Will was a darling among Episcopal circles; he had made so many appearances and spoken to so many Episcopal gatherings that Episcopalians began to think of him as one of their own. For this reason, he took to handing out business cards that read something to the effect that he was not currently nor had he ever been an Episcopalian. (One can't help but observe that the same was true of Jesus!) Will had given

Bob some good advice when Bob confessed that he was exhausted with civil rights sit-ins and Vietnam marches. Will had said to Bob that he was not so important to the cause that he had to be at every event in order for the cause to be won. Oh, and by the way, the last time we saw Will, he was speaking at an Episcopal conference here in Little Rock.

There is, in the box, a white rose. It is intact, the stem having been cut to fit the box exactly. Set beneath it is a note in Bob's hand: "This is the rose Annie held on the happiest night of my life." I had carried a single white rose when we married. Bob Cooper was the best thing that ever happened to me—just outright the best. I was like a half-born child, and without him in my life, I might never have been whole. As I said earlier, he would say that I had given him to himself. If that is true, what a lovely gift I gave. Something that is without doubt true is that the entrance of one into the life of the other created an enormous upheaval in both of us. We came away from that encounter being entirely different people than what we had thought ourselves to be—and for the better. As Bob had said of it, we were murdering our own souls in trying to fit into something that either was outgrown or was the wrong pattern to follow in the first place or, I would add a third: something that we had messed up so badly that there was nothing to do but bring it to an end.

The last item in the box is one that I placed there after Bob's passing—the stone that he carried in his pocket for so many years that it is worn smooth. I had never known him to be without it. And when the time comes to place his ashes in the ground, I hope it is remembered to put this stone among them. I think I will find a little pouch and tie it around the neck of the urn that contains his ashes. That and a pocketknife because, after all, "It is a poor man who doesn't have a pocketknife," he'd said. Both the knife and the stone stayed on his bedside table when he was ill.

What is not in the box, and what I wish I could find to place there, is a touching gift that Bob brought me when he returned from spring break that senior year. It was a purple-ish rose that he picked from the garden of Joye Pregnall when he visited her and Bill in Berkeley. He had placed it in a tobacco tin and brought it back in his briefcase. He knew how I found delight in roses, and even though it had been days since it had been in the garden, it was still lovely. It wasn't just the rose; it was the knowledge that I had been thought of. Another treasure far too large to fit into the box is an edition of The Jerusalem Bible illustrated by Salvador Dali and inscribed by me:

Robert Marsh Cooper

31 December 1985
the 25th anniversary
of his ordination to
the priesthood

With great delight I sit in
His shadow
And his fruit is sweet to
My taste

The lines of poetry are not mine; they are lines from the Song of Solomon 2:3 (AH-C).

I have written a long time today, and I am so very tired, weary through to my soul. Memories, sweet though they may be, are not always easy things to steep oneself in overlong. I am exhausted and a bit sad. I must turn my mind to other things.

As Bob would also say, "It's time to fly up to the roost."

CHAPTER 18

The Vow*

All the ways
you surprise me
love me
All the ways

—Robert Cooper[35]

This memory is one of the eruptions of the spirit of the Divine in the lives of two desperate and ordinary people—desperate because we were losing hope for ourselves, and ordinary because what was happening to us goes on every day in the lives of countless people who are more like us than not.

When Bob and I married, we included in the vows the phrase "With my body I thee worship." It went like this: "With this ring I thee wed, with my body I thee worship. With all that I am, and all that I have, I honor you, in the Name of the Father, and of the Son, and of the Holy Spirit." Including that phrase, "With my body I thee worship," was just the kind of thing that two smart-alecky, overly educated people would do. I don't know whose idea it was initially; but we were both pleased with the idea.

* An earlier draft of this chapter appeared by permission of this author in *Crossing the Owl's Bridge* by Kim Bateman, PhD, and published by Chiron in 2016.

The phrase came from one of the most ancient prayer books in the Anglican tradition,* and we had knowingly taken it completely out of context. In that era, it meant that a man was designating this woman to be his wife, not his concubine, and he was placing a ring on her finger to designate that to one and all. But Bob and I were doing it for entirely different reasons. We had discovered in each other an excitement and creativity in our sexuality that we had not known before. We wanted to celebrate it and nurture it. What we were doing was vowing that we would not lose it by neglect or to the kinds of resentments that can spring up between two people and close them off from each other.

You Know Why This Is Yours

I wear it a goncet about my neck
use it as amulet the string of kisses
the nipples you sucked made me your nurse
learned from me about "the breasts of kings"
your mouth the salt you licked you taste the wreck
of my flesh and your each small bite releases
more than I thought left of me to rehearse
the long tale we tell of the reckonings
our vast bodies yet have unknown to come
to the countings of delight our dusts are
when each moist breath measures how far
still we are from what may be the sum
of the ways you teach us how to praise
fragile flesh how few how lovely its days
(Cooper)[36]

When a loved one is diagnosed with some form of dementia, the first thing a spouse or child tries to do is keep the one they love looking presentable to the world, but they will eventually fail. Then later there is the struggle to keep them looking presentable to friends who stop by, and there to, they fail as well. In the end, the struggle is to keep the sense of

---

* Phrase taken from the 1662 Anglican Book of Common Prayer, having changed the word Ghost to Spirit.

being presentable alive in their loved one themselves. The latter, with time, becomes as impossible as the former two. People fail and falter, and as they do, they become more and more horrified by themselves. Bob said to me one day, "I am going mad, and I must not take you with me."

It is said that empathy is one of the things that goes away with dementia, and it is true. But if you begin with great amounts of empathy, and if that empathy has been instinctive all your lifelong, then some of that instinct will remain for a time. Such was the case with Bob. While his ability to see things through the eyes of others was increasingly diminished, he still cared about what his actions created in the lives of others, especially when those actions were visible to him.

As the years passed, Bob had less and less control of himself and certainly of life. The mechanisms that had readily gotten food to his mouth or brushed his teeth grew slack along with everything else. Then one terrible day when what I suppose we all fear the most about our loss of control had happened, Bob stood over me, leaning heavily on his walker, as I, on hands and knees, cleaned the soiled bathroom floor. He said in the most grieved voice, a voice choked and laden with sadness that came from the deepest parts of his soul, "Annie, my princess." Then he paused as he tried to find his voice and started again, "My princess, I never in all my life intended that you should have to be doing something like this—never—never."

I am not sure what I was thinking in the moment just before he spoke. When a loved one is ill like this, every day brings something new that one must do for them. I was living life for two people. Whatever I did for myself, I did for him. Two meals to be eaten. Two baths to be taken. Two heads to be combed. Two. Two. Two. Two. I would find myself caught between fatigue and mindless, rote behaviors. I am quite sure that at times I showed little emotion—just blunted responses and reactions. And I dared not think of what the next day might hold for us. For the first time in my life, I had come to fear the future.

It is said, perhaps carelessly so, that dementia destroys souls. I am not at all sure that this is true; in fact, I doubt it seriously. But certainly something is being destroyed, and it is not just the one diagnosed with dementia who is afflicted. Bob had feared that he would take me into madness with him, and his fear had not been entirely unfounded. But when I heard him speak that day, I was completely taken out of that self-involved place. The pain, shame, and sorrow in his voice was not a pain that I could have ignored had I tried. Nor could I have let his concern for me go unheard.

In that split second, I was standing with Bob before friends and family on our wedding night. We were on a balcony looking out over the canyon as the sun set, Bob so handsome in his linen jacket. We were so happy. I heard the vow that I had made decades before and then had almost entirely forgotten. It had struck me now with a fresh and powerful meaning.

I stopped what I was doing, looked up at Bob, and said with a strong, clear voice that came from somewhere deep inside, so deep that it seemed not to be my own, "Bobby, with my body, I thee worship." Everything shifted in that moment. The most beatific smile came over Bob's face; he remembered! Disease had not robbed him of that memory. Those words made our circumstances as close to comfortable for him as they possibly could. For that moment, his shame was gone.

For me, I received a renewed sense of purpose and courage—that second wind that runners talk about. That day, by God's mercy, I found the truth in the claim that we can stand almost anything, perhaps all things, if we can find meaning in them. Tending to Bob had now taken on a sacramental quality. That vow and the remembrance of it carried both of us through to the end. I have been blessed, and it has been Bob's love and care on that and other sad, sweet days that became such a blessing. I would not give back a single day of our life together. Every piece fit another, the good days and the bad, the happy and the sad; it all came together in the end to become a glorious thing. There has to have been some Divine force behind it all; left on our own, even with our best efforts, it would have been a botched mess—and that is a certainty.

CHAPTER 19

The Mystical Stairway

... one man loved the pilgrim soul in you,
And loved the sorrows of your changing face

—Yeats "When You are Old"

Slow deaths are terrible things. It seems that we said goodbye so many times along the way. Goodbye to Bob being the manager of the bills and insurance payments and all the many things he had done for us, for me. Goodbye to Bob the driver, errand runner, and grocery shopper. Goodbye to Bob who had enjoyed the symphony and art exhibits. Goodbye to travel when Bob no longer wanted to leave home. As time passed, he was so often carefree that I would find myself, in those moments when I was insane with responsibility, envying him for having become childlike. I was forgetting those horrible times when he was preoccupied with how to find his way out of life.

Over the years of his illness, there had been various phases. Initially he was furious, mostly with me because I most often crossed his path, but before he was done, he had had an angry episode with just about everybody. It never lasted long, and sometimes it was forgotten by him, literally, before I could even realize what had happened. Other times, he would tear into me as I left for my office, and then, by the time I got there, he would have left a message on the phone filled with self-hatred and remorse, berating himself for having treated me so poorly. It was all so bewildering—to both of us.

The end to these rages came when he was finally diagnosed and I had moved my work home. It was then that he seemed to simply make peace with his illness, though I was never quite sure whether he knew exactly what was headed our way. Bob was sometimes blessed and sometimes cursed with the gift of denial. In this case, it was a gift.

When the anger passed, he became so dear. The people who would come to help me care for him would comment on how kind he was. This was the Bob that I had known before the tension around his illness had disrupted it. That is certainly not to say that that is how he was known to all people. Bob could be a one-man army if he got his passions to a high pitch, but that had never before been aimed at me. Also, it never was fully unleashed at me; it was just the shock of the shift that had stunned and hurt me so. The sweetness, once it returned, never went away, thank God. I recall that Jan, his nurse, said one day after his bath that she did not know what we were going to do when he stopped caring about what made things good for his Annie. He would resist doing things until it was explained that it would make my life easier if he would do them before the afternoon when I would be home alone with him; with that, he would willingly take action. In that way, he looked out for me to the end.

This resistance usually took place around the taking of a bath and getting into fresh pajamas. We would try to give him as much control as possible by doing things like ask when he would want to bathe if the present moment was not it. He would say things like 10:34 a.m. That did not mean that he wanted to do it any more at 10:34, but it gave things a bit more of a playful quality around it. That is when he would be reminded by someone, and not in my presence, that it would be harder on me physically if the chore were left to afternoon when I would have to help him maneuver, just the two of us without added assistance.

Then, though the kindness remained, periods of profound confusion began. To a considerable extent, these episodes of extreme disarray were driven by delusions that followed a pattern. He had developed a disorder called sleep behavioral disorder. He had frightening dreams of a repetitive sort. Some of these dreams had gone on at least as long as I had known him—the forgotten lecture, the missed flight, losing his place in the Prayer Book during a service, but now these had taken on a frightening nightmarish quality. To these were added disaster dreams. Then came the terrible truth that the medication that would treat this disorder would worsen the dementia, and medication for the dementia would worsen the dreams. He struggled on without medication for either disorder. He was trapped in a body that was betraying him at every turn. He knew he was in misery, but he understood none of the complexities of that.

Bess and Rebecca were good about calling or sending cards, but the grandchildren were now in their twenties and less prone to get on the phone, though they would text. Because Bob had largely lost his sense of time, I did not worry about this. Then one day he began to name those voices from whom he had not heard. He looked up at me in horror and asked, "Are they all dead?" That night, his fear worked its way into his early dreams. I was still up waiting for the person who would come to relieve me. Bob came wandering back out into the hall, where I met him. He thought that Bailey had wandered out into the night looking for Charlie. I assured him that all was well and that he did not have to worry. He was too tired to search for her in the house. I think that much of the time he thought of her as still that little urchin banging away for the quartz with his geologist's pick and wearing her oversized goggles. From that point forward, I made more effort to keep him in touch with everyone.

One horrible night, fairly early on, before he lost so much of his physical strength, he had gotten into the coat closet where the vacuum was stored and unzipped the bag, thinking that it was his carry-on. The mad traveler was trying to pack for a trip when Rebecca, who was visiting, was roused from sleep. She, joined by me, struggled to ease him from this terrible sense that he had a trip to make, another speech to deliver, or another committee to sit on. We never told him he was wrong; instead we persuaded him to go back to sleep, and we would help in the morning. By morning, things were forgotten because some other bad dream had taken its place. What enormous relief there was for me to know that it was not time for him to leave, not yet. I still had not come to a place where I could bear to let him go, even though I knew that to remain lengthened his struggles.

One evening he was swinging a lamp around, thinking it was a telephone that was out of order. When I eased him back into bed after that particularly wild episode, he looked at me in one of those brief lucid moments that frequently came on the heels of sheer madness and said, "How can we make the best of this, and how can I be a part of that?" I asked him where his heart was, and he tapped over my heart as he had done so many times before. Then I tapped his chest and said that he could help by carrying my heart carefully, and I would do the same for him. He asked if that would be forever, and I assured him it would be.* He relaxed, and it was not long before he drifted off to sleep. Sitting in that darkened room, I could only hope that that was the end of the bedlam for the night and that he would sleep soundly. After one of these episodes, I was always so amazed by how frightening it was, not just for him but for me as well. It was as if I were being sucked into the delirium myself—as if my hold on reality was a tenuous one at best. Partly this was because these episodes tended to happen in the night, and I would have been awakened from a sound sleep. But there was something more.

One of the books that Bob and I had read together was entitled *The Psychotic Core*. It's author is Michael Eigen. We, Bob and I, had thought so much of the book that Bob suggested that it be read and discussed by the staff where he was executive director. On this night, as on many other occasions, I thought of the "psychotic core" and wondered just how closely we all skate toward the edge of madness without taking it seriously until we are so close to being drawn into its vortex. I wondered what that author would have had to say about it, had he been there with us, watching what was happening. Were we sliding off into some *participation mystique?*

When Bob told me there was writing on the wall in Greek or Hebrew but that he could not make it out no matter how hard he squinted, a chill would come over me. When he saw people walking in the hallway in dark coats and hats, it was unnerving. If he thought that there were thieves in the house or in an imaginary hotel room and that we were being robbed blind, I did not know what to do to help him aside from placing calls to a psychologist friend of mine, Denise Compton. She would then become whomever she needed to be on the other end of the line, listening to his story and assuring him that something would be done immediately to stop the problem. It always worked!

Along about this time, Bob developed a delusional obsession that was not so hard to understand; there was even a dearness about it. Bob had grown up in a two-story house, and he would ask me from time to time how many floors were in this house—one. Later he had begun to look for what

---

* We were acting out the poem of e. e. cummings, as we often had before.

he called "the mystical stairway." For years, he would get out of bed and begin the search. I helped, but Bob also conscripted all caregivers, our girls, guests, anyone he could find to participate in the search for this magical place. As he stood just behind me, we would open the closet door and peer closely down that wall to see if we could find the spot that gave onto this magnificent place. Not finding it there, we would look behind the bookcase and then back again from the opposite corner. We would go to the adjoining room and look down and up again on the reverse side of the wall. Bob had a hard time finding things even in the best of times, and if he lost something, he could not adopt my method of just waiting and letting things present themselves. I had come across lost items in the most inexplicable places, and I was persuaded that helpful angels were behind it all. But no, Bob had to find it *now* or just nearly drive himself nuts obsessing over it. As a consequence, I had become his official "finder upper" because that was far easier than watching him agonize over it. So if I had found things when he was a well man, he expected that I would be able to do this still. When I could not turn up the mystical stairway, he would be so disappointed in me; I had let him down. He would take it in stride as best he could and crawl back into bed to lie in wait for the next person who might not be so inept, though he never said it that way. I knew he was searching for a way out of this life. I knew he was tired. He was looking for a way home. I was going to have to come to grips with this and let him go. I knew too that these fantastical trips and the stairway were signs that he was on his way, but he always insisted that I go with him. We just kept looking until he concluded, or seemed to, that the stairway was not yet ready to be revealed. Then we would resume the search the next time he thought of it. I never once tried to tell him that those stairs did not exist; I just apologized for being unable to find them. I believed they were there—maybe not to be seen by mundane eyes but there nonetheless.

As I have explained before, a good bit of time, his ultimate solution for avoiding exhausting travel was to have the house move. We would set down next door to Ed and Trully Safrit in Hendersonville or near his boyhood home with the pink and white dogwood in bloom. I rather enjoyed the fantasies too, and I could recognize the vague outline of things we had actually done before. We had visited Ed and Trully when Bob had a speaking engagement nearby, and we had been there when there was a dusting of snow on the rhododendron blossoms. We had also made a point of being with his mother when the dogwood trees in her lawn had bloomed. Bob had found a way for us to do that again—not that there was any conscious intention in it; his thinking was too disorganized for that. We made visits somewhere most every morning, during that period when he was most likely to think that the house had traveled overnight. He once remarked how lucky we were to have the house with us no matter where we went. He was full of wonder at this phenomenon. We were making the best of it where we could.

There were other trips though—frightening ones when he thought that we were on a cruise and that he had gotten separated from me and precious-dog-Charlie. The ship was going down, and he could not find us. He suffered with these. They began after we had people staying with him at night. We had brought them into our household because he was beginning to get his days and nights turned about and would not let me sleep. Consequently, I was sleeping in our bedroom with Charlie, and Bob was going to bed in his library, where we had placed a hospital bed. He was surrounded by all his books and paintings, much as they had been in his seminary office. A spare bedroom was close by his library so that his assistants could nap there and rouse at the sound of his walker. But he would wake up and find me missing; this would unwind him.

If the night person was resourceful enough, she would help him leave me a note under the bedroom door and then get him distracted with cookies or ice cream or pizza that they had saved from the evening before. Anything else he ate had to be "fixed up" with picante sauce. Whether it was pork loin or roast beef, it needed picante and maybe even some salt. I would learn that dementia distorts taste; sugar and salt are among the few things that can be tasted most easily. In Bob's case, it also included jalapeños!

So, happily fed and feeling physically spent again, Bob would usually head back to his bed and sleep a bit more. If the night person was less resourceful or if his spell was particularly bad, I would be back up again and hoping that the next night would be a more peaceful one for us all. Not long after his death, I found one of these notes again. Many of the words are illegible, but basically it said that he was frightened that I was hurt and I should telephone him. Then there was a plea that I call immediately. When I had read that the next morning, my heart sank. One terrible part about caregiving is that you never come to a place where you feel that you have done all you should do—or even that you have done all that you can do. I had to decide every morning when I awoke that I would forgive myself in advance for all the things that I failed to get right that day.

These ideas of travel and separation and the mystical stairway went on for years, but one afternoon not long before the end, something unique happened, and nothing remotely like it ever occurred again. Bob asked me if I had enough money. "Do you have enough money?" he said. At first I thought it was just another prelude to his concern that we were going to be traveling, or were already traveling; he had an anxiety of running out of enough cash on trips real or imagined. It had become such a source of anxiety that I had taken to keeping some bills in his money clip near his bed so that I or someone could show it to him when his apprehensions arose. Because I thought it another of those times, I asked him if he was concerned that *we* had enough money. But no, he was in a very lucid moment, and before I could reach for his money clip, he corrected me: "No, I said do *you* have enough money." I was stunned. This was new territory. He was concerned about my future and my finances—a future that did not include him. "Yes, Bobby, I have plenty of money," and it was the truth. This was asked without there yet being any obvious signs that the end was so near, but I had a strong intuition that he was getting ready to go. But, before I continue the telling of our parting I want to remind the reader who might be jarred by Bob's last words to me that he was never a slave to convention and he was true to himself to the end. I do not know what you will read; but what I heard were familiar words of love and devotion. To have changed his last words would have been to betray his integrity. In his poetry had written that he wanted his next to the last word to be freedom and for the last to be yes. I believed this to be exactly what he was conveying. He had also said that he wanted to be alive until he was dead.

Things would change in just hours; if the staircase were to be found, Bob was going to find it on his own. In the end, I don't recall that we said goodbye in those words, though we did not flinch in the face of it either. I assured him that I was safe and that he was free to go when he wanted to, that he had done a good job of making sure that I would have all I needed and beyond. He had given me those things that we both treasured the most and that would last forever. He was tired and would smile weakly and touch my face. He spoke very little, but his last words to me were uttered at the end of a long period of lucidity just before he slipped into silence. And he was my dearest Bob to the end. "Annie." Then motioning me to bend closer, he spoke his last words to me in a tender, loving voice. He sounded so young again as he said, "I still want to fuck you." Then as I held his hand, he drifted off to sleep and ultimately into some semiconscious state. It was Valentine's Day; a heart-shaped balloon was bobbing at the foot of his bed. For the three remaining days, I told him I loved him over and over again. I have never stopped. Love still passes between us.

It is comforting and sustaining to know that, despite all our struggles and indignities along the way, a tenderness passed from him to me and back and forth again—it is without end. The magic that I had so feared losing to the routine of marriage had not eluded us—faltered sometimes—but never lost sight of.

AH'S

At the end of November
I could see you through the not yet
bare trees sitting in the moon's lap
between here and Saturn and Venus
in the southwestern sky

Still across that distance

We both heard the laughter of our unborn
child in the long room of our hearts.
(Cooper)[37]

Now as I look back, I think how he often had his eye on the skies—rooted in the earth, oh yes, but looking upward. I'm thinking what a lovely thing to seek—a mystical stairway; and sometimes when I am in that room lined with his books, I glance down the wall to see if perhaps he has left something tied to a handrail so that I might be able to grasp it and find my way to him. But I suppose things like that do not emerge from the mists of unconsciousness until it is time to find the way. And I also understand why he sought it long before it was time for him to climb. Until my end comes, I must satisfy myself with the echo of laughter in "the long room of our hearts" and thank God for it with all my being.

CHAPTER 20

The Bumper Sticker

Set me as a seal upon thine heart,
Set me as a seal upon thine arm,
For love is strong as death.
Many waters cannot quench love,
Neither can the floods drown it.

—Song of Solomon 8:6–7 King James Version

Bob detested bumper stickers because, he claimed, no sentiment worth having or policy worth supporting could be reduced to so few words. He never interpreted a heart shape; he always read it aloud as "I heart New York" or whatever else someone was "hearting." This was not a new position for him; he had held it long before I arrived on the scene. And he made no secret of his opinion either. I heard him speak of how his students had heard it so often that they had taken to teasing him by putting bumper stickers on his office door. If Bob had a position, it was held passionately, so the best one of them that appeared on his door said, "You have mistaken me for someone who cares." He loved that one—spoke of it often.

Sometimes when Bob and I went to Dallas or Fort Worth, it was to see exhibits at the various museums in the area; at other times, Bob had speaking engagements. We would combine these with visits to my sister Sharon and her family, John and daughter, Jenny, who lived in the suburbs at that time. In the earlier years the Bels lived in the city, and we exchanged visits with them. The most bizarre evening we spent in Dallas was with Ernest on the evening just after Bob's father's death. Initially we had gone to Henderson, Texas, to visit my father, whose birthday was on the thirtieth of December. The next morning, Bob and I were out running some errands when the call came. When we got back, Papa, who had a clear liking for Bob, said that Gary had called. Bob asked if it was about his dad; Papa said it was. Then the next question, "Is he gone?" Yes he was. I thought it all so incongruous. These two men had only just met, struck a bond, and then suddenly my father was telling Bob of his father's death. Then Papa, who was not a demonstrative man, put his arm around Bob's shoulders and gave Bob an awkward squeeze. It was a faint motion, but just for a second, I saw Bob let his weight sink into that awkward embrace. And then we were back to business. The plan had been to drive to Dallas that afternoon to go to a New Year's Eve party at the Bels'. The weather was turning bad fast, and the ice was beginning to form on the roads. There were two choices for flights to Charlotte—Dallas and Shreveport; Bob chose Dallas because that would not move me farther from home and I would be staying in a warm, inviting place, not a hotel, while I waited for the thaw so I could drive myself home. I threw things into suitcases as Bob made reservations for his flight. There would be none until the next day, if then. In less than half an hour, we took our quick leave, and off we went, racing the weather to the interstate in the belief that once on it, the trucks would have kept it clear. Wrong. It was an awful drive, but hours later, we made it to the Bels' home.

Bob was not ready to let his father go. When we had left days before, I asked if he should not take his topcoat in the event that he would have to go to North Carolina. I remember exactly what he said, "Well, if I do, I'll just be SOL." He simply did not believe it could happen, at least not just then, and now that it had, he had been embraced by a near stranger and taken in by friends. That night, Bob and I put on our party clothes, went downstairs, said hello to a few friends, scared up something to eat in the kitchen, and made our way back upstairs. I remember regretting that I would never meet Bob's father and that that would be a loss we would not be able to compensate for. The other thing I thought was how classy it was "to shuffle off this mortal coil" (as Shakespeare had had Hamlet put it) on the last day of the year when one had Father Time as a traveling companion.

Father it is Your Birthday

I had thought until today
that you would not die
would live forever

but it comes over me now
like the dusk of Northern winter
suddenly

I had thought this to frustrate
time   to castrate Chronos
the fear washing away my own aging
sands   washing at the shores
of the darkness crouching behind my birth and yours

I find that I can fashion
nothing to give the lie
to this   to stay the hands
that confirm our common clay
(Cooper)[38]

The next morning, Bob, dressed against the weather as best he could in brown slacks and a wool tweed sport coat that he had bought decades before in Edinburgh, boarded a flight for Charlotte—SOL. In his hand he carried a copy of Pat Conroy's *Prince of Tides* that Ernest had located on his library shelf and handed to Bob on his way out the door. A man from one crazy southern family handing another man from another crazy southern family a book about an even crazier southern family. That night, Bob slept in the same bed he had slept in as a boy. During the night, he was awakened by what he thought were voices rising up the stairwell from the floor below. He started down the stairs to see who it was and realized that his mother's voice was raised in anger. The bickering that had gone on between his mother and father in this life was continuing into the next. Bob said a terrible fatigue came over him and that it persisted until the morning after the burial, when he began working off his sorrow, chopping to bits branches that had fallen in the ice storm that had moved across the South. As Bob worked with his back and arms, Gary was dealing with the cemetery and funeral home, because their father had been buried in the wrong plot. Mabel Cooper had realized the error immediately, but for the sake of propriety, she had remained quiet until only family members were present. I recall the weight in Bob's voice that night when we talked on the phone. "Dad couldn't even get it right from the grave." In the early days of Bob's illness, he would attempt to bate me, and there were times when I took it, but once I simply said I was not going to play Mabel to his Bob, and he backed off immediately.

Over the years, Bob had spoken of the bickering between his parents, but I had taken it for just that. But just as Bob and I were falling in love, he did two things. The first occurred when I was taking a strong stand about something, just as we had always done with each other over the years. Suddenly Bob backed down, just withered. I asked him what had just happened. I don't think he even recognized what had passed between us. I told him that I enjoyed being with him because he was a worthy opponent and that if he was going to withdraw his intellect and strong will, the pleasure of being around him would go with it. He began to stay with the argument as he always had before we had fallen in love. This ability to keep the debate going was one of the great delights of our life together until he lost his way with dementia and could no longer sort out the serious from the playful. The claims about which was the best, Texas beef barbeque or North Carolina pulled pork were no longer fun, much less a debate about who came closest to hitting the mark, Jung or Freud or some theological topic. Rather than being fun, these conversations became something that could cause upset and confusion.

The second thing occurred when Bob took responsibility for something I had done. He apologized to me, claiming fault when he did not have any fault in it at all. I was the one in the wrong, and I was sure of it. Once again, the air went out of the room. We agreed that day that I would carry my own shadow. When I was wrong, I needed and wanted to be held responsible for it; I did not want to fall into that horrible southern pattern of "if Mama ain't happy, ain't nobody happy." It is just sick, and it destroys relationships and marriages and families. Nobody wins in the end. I grew up with that, and I know what comes of it. But both of us had to have been caught up in these old, old patterns earlier in our lives before we could have had enough experience or wisdom to identify something as problematic and recognize it when it arose.

This worked well for us until the dementia weakened the functions of his frontal lobes; then he was cruel, responsible for nothing, and I was wrong all the time. There is no way to describe how wearing this was for me. Often he had no desire for forgiveness and likely no memory of what had transpired between us except for some sour sense in him that something had gone wrong. That was the worst time of our lives. Eventually, even the vague remorse for these events went away. I was highly suspicious of what was happening, I thought such a personality change had to be organic, but by the time we had a diagnosis, I had made up my mind that if that were not so, I would have to question my own sanity for exposing myself to such brutal (in a verbal sense only) treatment. I was going to have to come to grips with whether I should stay or go.

He had to have known that something was wrong, and my pleas for him to get help just inflamed his fears and fury. But once we knew what was happening, love reigned again. I guess it always had, or we would have given up—but life now was not as hard, as strange as that must sound. I do not mean that the demands of his care were not great, but these mostly grew from love, and they were usually accepted in love. That made it all so much easier. To the very end, making my life better was his chief concern—that and his concern for the well-being of family. Knowing his devotion made me so happy. And my goal? It was his contentment. I measured every decision by that.

In those hours when I feel overwhelmed by grief, I pull out my list of all the things that Bob gave me and add to it. It will be endless; the gifts of self and soul are without end, and material things given are many as well. Gratitude overtakes grief almost invariably. I walk about our home, and I touch the things that are ours and remember with thankfulness. Bob loved the lushness of his environment; he surrounded himself with books, art, books, sculpture, books, crystal, and just a few more books. But he was generous and lived open-handedly. If you are a panhandler, you want to find a Bob Cooper. The troubled gathered outside the church door waiting for Father, because Father was going to empty his pockets into theirs. If you were a charity or manning a kettle outside the grocery store at Christmastime, you were looking for a Coop. If you were hopeless, filthy, and sitting on a New York street, you could count on it being Bob Cooper's hand that appeared within your reach, offering a hot dog. If you were a wild schizophrenic on the streets of Boston, it would be Bob who found where you slept under the portico of the Unitarian Church and every morning, thereafter, left a cup of coffee on a nearby step, staying just far enough away so as not to threaten you. And every evening, it would be that same Bob who prayed for you, referring to you as "our brother" and thinking of you on your cardboard box when he was in his own warm bed. Bob's heart went out to those on the margins.

People had presumed early in his career in the church that Bob would rise to the top, but he had made too many enemies and spoken his opinions emphatically too often. He ultimately realized that these aspirations were not his, at least not anymore. Toward the end of his years of service, when someone heard that Cooper had agreed to be the priest in charge of the smallest and poorest of churches in a part of Little Rock that had been abandoned to violence and the lowliest of souls by all but a few dedicated congregants, this person said that it was a complete misfit. He could not have known Bob very well. Bob had always felt called to the edges, and now, finally, after years of hard work, he had the financial freedom to follow that call to the downtrodden. In some important ways, that was what much of his work in Florida had been.

The Greeks said that none but the gods and wild beasts could live outside the city walls. To a great extent, Bob was one who did just that—lived outside the city walls. I think he was a bona fide shape-shifter, being here an erudite Greek and there a clown—here an angel and there a wild beast. In the end, it would be these dear people at Good Shepherd who would support Bob with their love and understanding to his last day on earth and beyond. I am indebted to them all for their care. I love each one. But I was thinking about bumper stickers, wasn't I.

On one of our return trips from Dallas, Bob pulled in for gasoline and, of course, a Baby Ruth. While I tried to walk around and stretch the kinks out of my car-weary bones, Bob browsed the rack of bumper stickers. Bob and bumper stickers? I thought the world had shifted on its axis. Then I saw what the one he was holding said: "When I Die Bury Me Upside Down, So Everybody Can Kiss My Ass." Now it all made sense. The wild beast was loose in the truck stop. Bob put that sticker on his own office door. He bought two that day, but I had no idea what he planned to do with the second. He likely intended to send it to someone, but then the candidates for it must have been too many to ever make a decision. I came across it the other day tucked away in a box.

When Bob's end was nearing, he moved into a week of lucidity. Suddenly he was himself day after day. He had lost the use of his legs not long before. Now I was seeing the signs of the end that I had become conscious of when I was working with dying patients. Hospice was called in. The disparity of our sizes, Bob's and mine, did make it hard for me—that I was willing to admit—but it was worth the risk to me just so that we could have the privacy that we had enjoyed in our afternoons together; I did not want to lose that. It is hard to be constantly surrounded by others. As lovers, we had lost so much already, but time to speak of love in the quiet of our own home was too great a loss to bear. I would eventually pay the price, but I would pay it again for the joy of our time together.

The last Sunday that Bob was conscious, he preached a sermon with me as his sole congregant. It went on for forty-five minutes and was vintage Bob Cooper, far from intellectually polished or erudite as in the past, but it was all there. Some of it I recognized from his Stewart Lectures that he had been so pleased with but for which he could never find a publisher. When he had finished, I asked what had inspired him to preach, and he said in his slow, wonderful drawl, "Oh, our life together."

Over the next few days, he did well. When I say he was lucid, I mean the lucidity of the dying. He was in the real world, able to talk and answer questions reasonably, but he was also becoming more and more absorbed by the souls of the saints "who walk in the light" (BPC). When I would sit quietly with him in the afternoons, he would greet people, unseen by me, as they entered the room. He would laugh and talk about various forms of mischief they had been party to. During none of that time did he address someone whose name I recognized, though others were present when he spoke with his father and brother, Jim, who had preceded him in death. None of us heard him speak to his mother or Terry and Will, for whom he had grieved so painfully. At times he would ask how many were in the room. The first time, I made the mistake of saying that only Charlie and I were with him. He looked so confused; then I realized that he was seeing others and not those chilling forms in black coats and hats of those darker days. From then on, when he repeated the query, I simply said that I suspected there were many; but he would have to tell me, not I him. That seemed to satisfy him. On one occasion, he told me there were people and angels with us. You must understand, I describe him as lucid because I believe these experiences to be real. Time and again, I have stood at the bed of the dying and had them introduce me to those who were visible to me and those who were not. I have come to the conclusion that as we move toward what we call death, we become conscious of a wider world than we can comprehend when saddled with the illusions of the physical world. Bob was also aware of the angels. Rilke had called angels terrible "birds of the soul" (*Duino Elegies*). So these awe-filling creatures were with us, and I trusted them to know the way now. Soon I would have to yield my care of Bob to them, and it was this that I feared, not the angels themselves. I found their presence comforting—these vast mothering-fathering beings.

On that last Valentine's Day, before he fell asleep, I spent a little bit of time reminding Bob of a particularly wonderful Valentine's evening that we had spent over a fine dinner in a small restaurant within walking distance of our Florida condo. The ceiling was covered in red, white, and silver Mylar balloons. To get to our table, we made our way through a forest of streamers. The movement of people about the room would create waves of the balloons and streamers above the space where diners were seated. What a lovely evening; being wildly in love is a wonderful thing. Now on this last Valentine's evening, that love had been tested and had not been found wanting. And while I was the only one who did any talking, Bob smiled and began to relax. I held his hand as he fell asleep. In the morning, he was unresponsive. I would never hear his wonderful voice again, not from this world.

It was beginning to snow again. It was so quiet. Quiet as a tomb. We were alone. I pulled Terry's book from the shelf and read Bob's poem again. Terry introduces it by telling how the poem came about. He and Bob had been talking about death and of their mutual longing for the South and how it was missed in the northern winters. Then Terry had turned to Bob and said that he did not want to be buried under all that snow. Later that evening, Bob wrote the poem, and Terry had asked to use it. It is in a book dedicated to Bob and two other friends, Ernest Bel and Joe Morris Doss, all of Louisiana days.

Say When the Dying Is Done

Say, when the thing is done—
  My dying—
that I fell softly like an early snow
from an undetermined height.
I would have told you if I could
that the wind declining is a blow
  suffered with pleasure,
that I awoke as a man does—
O, thankful—from a dream of falling

Dream-sifted through reveries of other days
sleep-dropped through darkness of cool sheets,
and mother-comfort comes to hold you.

I would have told you if I could.

And let it not be said that he was one
howling like a whipped dog in the tunneled night,
limping cradling the broken bones he cannot mend,
that he ran off to lick new wounds by old light,
to nurse his raw life—his darkness—that doesn't end.

I would have told you, what I cannot know,
that I fell softly like an early snow.
(Cooper)[39]

I had long thought that it would be snowing when Bob stepped beyond this world. It was a strange thing, living in Texas and then Florida, to be thinking this way. It was not a new sense, this knowing of how it would be for him when he died. I think that the first inkling came upon me when he read to me this poem way back when I was a student sitting in his office. But as the years went past, this knowing grew stronger and stronger. It wasn't a scary thing, just a quiet acknowledgment of some faint truth. It had snowed so much all that winter, but Bob had been strong enough for me to believe that he would be with us for a good deal longer. It had never occurred to me at Christmas that that would be our last one. But now was different. I felt like the time had grown very near. That was a Friday night.

When nothing had changed for the better on Sunday, I knew that the time was near. That afternoon, while Bob was quiet in his bed, I took his alb from the closet and washed it one more time. I could imagine how we were going to get his jeans on and his shirt, but given his size and the volume of his alb, I could not see how we could move him about successfully. I had a plan. I laid the alb out on a bed and began the process of snapping and tying the front into place; then I blind stitched the front opening closed. Next I placed it on the ironing board and pinked up the back from the hem to the collar, taking care to keep the hood out of the way; I folded and stitched back the raw edges. As I did this, I thought of the countless times I had seen him wearing this alb, celebrating the Eucharist at the altar of various churches or chapels. I thought of him at the wedding of Bess and Kirby. I thought of the madman-preacher striking flint as he stalked about the chapel with the alb billowing behind. I thought of Sundays at Ascension in Clearwater and now Little Rock at the cathedral or Good Shepherd. After all this grief and tears and nostalgia and pricked fingers came laughter—wild, uncontrollable laughter—hysteria more likely. "When I Die Bury Me Upside Down So Everybody Can Kiss My Ass." I hoped Bob knew he had always been and still was a source of great joy for me. Quirky, brilliant, funny Bobby, you are my soul's great delight.

By late afternoon, I was persuaded all the more that Bob had found his mystical stairway. Regina had come for her night shift. She is a soothing, quiet person, and she always brought peace with her. I had prayed that she would be with me at the end. I had somehow known that Bob would go in the night. The portents, like tumblers in a lock, were falling into place. I called Chris Keller and asked if he would come one more time, and he did. He stood at Bob's bed and prayed and then went with me into the next room, where he reminded me how to tie a cincture. After Chris left, I fell into bed. I have never been so tired. Regina had promised not to let Bob be alone and to wake me if anything began to change. But even with her reassurance, I could not sleep. I got into some jeans and a turtleneck, but before going back into Bob's room, I went outside in the cold. It was so quiet; there was a light snow swirling about me. I went in to be with Bob and told Regina to sleep, but she could not either. Weeks before, we had pulled the foot of Bob's bed out into the center of the room so that we could work with him from both sides; this didn't leave much open floor space. In that dimly lit room, I lay on the floor beneath his bed listening to his breathing as it became increasingly shallow. Every few minutes, I would rise to stroke his forehead and tell him I loved him and that I was nearby.

Bob became restless, and though we called hospice multiple times asking what we should do to help him, he just seemed to become more and more agitated with every dose of medication. We had not expected the hospice nurse when she arrived, but we were glad to see her. She could not get him settled either. I stayed with him, speaking often so that he knew I was there, but my attempts at quieting him were to no avail. The nurse asked if there was anyone to whom Bob had not said goodbye. He had said his goodbyes, or they had been said to him. Rebecca had called and sung him a song. Everyone else had sent him valentines. Then it struck me.

During his years of disorientation, he had often had that anxiety about Bailey's welfare. We would call and leave a message; she would respond, and he would be reassured again. What if now he had had a bad dream in which Bailey was frightened or in danger? I spoke of her to him, of her well-being, of how all was well with each of the kids. I saw him relax, and I watched the blood return to that great, warm heart as Bob made his way home knowing that the children were well. I looked up at the nurse and asked, already knowing the answer, "Is he gone?" Yes, he was. Now in the absence of Bob was this beautiful, lifeless form lying there in peace, having been spared a complete undoing. I must have told him a thousand times that night that I loved him. Now I found myself saying, "Bobby, we did it!" over and over again. By the grace of God, we had accomplished what we both wanted. He had died at home among his books and art, knowing who he was and never having forgotten his family or friends. He knew me, and he knew that he would be adored forever. I had this strange sense of elation like one who had run a nearly impossible race and won. I knew the sensation could not last long, but for that moment, it was good. I was so overwhelmed with gratitude that we had been given this magnificent gift. We have been blessed at every turn.

It was with sweet tenderness that we washed his body and placed the wooden cross of the Order of Holy Cross around his neck. He had worn it under his clothing for as long as I had known him and probably much before. As I sat nearby, Regina and the hospice nurse dressed him in the worn, faded jeans that he had liked the most. We slipped him into his softest chambray shirt and buttoned down the collar and chest pockets. Then came the alb; we shifted him from side to side and slid the newly sewn edges beneath him. Regina lifted his head again so that I could put the monk's hood in place between his shoulders. Then everyone stepped back as I knotted the cincture and put his priest's stole in its place, kissing the cross at the neck, the one he could no longer kiss for himself. As I did this, I saw the lovely remnants of his mother's linen and lace handkerchief that I had sewn on the neckline. Had there been a way on earth to get his boots on, we would have done it; but there was not, so we settled for second best—his Birkenstocks. Charlie jumped back up on the bed.

It seemed like only moments, and Lajean and Dari Hill were in the room. Rita Johnson was there in her bathrobe, holding me for dear life. Tim Guffey was planning meals. Sharon and John were there. It is all a blur now. Two very apologetic policemen asked a few routine questions and expressed their condolences. Jan arrived for her shift and was shaken by all the commotion in the street. A couple of quiet hours later, after persuading precious-dog-Charlie that he would have to jump down from his master's side, Bob's body was taken away. Jan and Regina began the process of "getting the sick out of the house." Those had been my words. I wanted the healthy Bob back, and I couldn't have him so long as we were still inundated with medical equipment. God bless them; they did it. I think that they finagled a kind man from hospice to help with things that were not remotely his problem. Lajean whisked me out of the house so that this work could be done. Sharon found a place where donations of hospital beds and other equipment were accepted; these people came quickly to pick things up. The rocking chair was brought down from the attic, and by the end of the day, the room was back to a library. The house was quiet again. I sat there in peace, a peacefulness that would not last long and, once gone, did not return for a very long time. But for those moments, Bob's spirit hung densely in the room as though he were hovering just above the windows. I love that space; it has never made me sad—contemplative but not sad. I begin my mornings there and return at sunset. In those early weeks, precious-dog-Charlie wouldn't enter the room; he came only as close as the threshold. Now he has his place behind my rocker where he does his devotionals. That first night, Sharon stayed with me and would have stayed much longer, but I wanted that first night behind me, the first night of being alone. The one I had dreaded so terribly and for so long that it was beginning to seem almost insurmountable.

> Keep watch, dear Lord, with those who work, or watch, or weep this night, and give thine angels charge over those who sleep. Tend the sick, Lord Christ; give rest to the weary, bless the dying, soothe the suffering, pity the afflicted, shield the joyous; and all for thy love's sake. Amen. (p. 71 BCP)

The funeral was going to have to wait for ten days before all could gather. Rebecca came a few days early to help me with whatever we had to do. I couldn't think of a thing, but she could. I had never planted pansies that year, but she found some somewhere and got them in the ground, explaining, "So you will look like yourself, Mother." Bess and Kirby arrived, and plans for a reception got into high gear. The day of the funeral, I looked around and saw that they were all there. Kirby, my children, grandchildren, their boyfriends, Sharon and John, my niece, Jenny and her husband, Wade, and their two sons, Benjamin, whom we call Ben, and Oliver. (Bob called them "the three-syllable boys.") I felt so loved and held by their devotion. They had all loved Bob and sat about spouting "Bobisms"—and always do when we gather. When we arrived at the cathedral, the bishop and clergy met us in the parlor. Prayers were offered, we walked in to the cathedral, and the service began.

Immediately after his death, I began tormenting myself trying to remember what Bobby looked like. Which thumb had that oddity? Which side the mole? It went on and on. I am not sure when relief began exactly. It did not happen all at once I know, but slowly those memories of him, of his body, began to come to the surface. It was a blessing, this forgetting, because now a strong, healthy body has emerged from the frail one. He stands tall and walks with a normal gait—well, almost normal. He had the slightest swing of his left foot. He wears aviator glasses again, and his teeth are crooked on the bottom, not all made perfect by the bridge that replaced the implanted ones of long ago. His hands are his hands again, including the right thumb with its strange crease; he called it "deformed." He smiles and laughs a lot. He speaks to me. I know his love.

One of our longest-running debates began when he preached at a wedding in the fall of 1984, and it went on for decades. The Hebrew Testament lesson was from Song of Solomon, "love is strong as death." I disagreed; I said love is stronger than death. In his preaching, Bob had taken the more traditional approach to the language. We were straining at gnats with that one, but the idea was fun, not some theological solution of importance. Well, I win, Bobby! Love is stronger than death. Love has won for us, and it will win every time. Oh, my dearest Bobby, I may miss your touch, but I am wrapped 'round in your love.

This part I always knew; there was no forgetting, not even of the temporary sort. When last I saw Bob, he was leaving this earth just as he had arrived here, "trailing clouds of glory" (Wordsworth, "Ode on Intimations of Immortality from Recollections of Early Childhood").

Everything Died Today

The man who had read
everything died today.
He was allowed to carry
none of his notes with him.
Only his hunch-backed memory
went along to the river.
Dutifully, he bore three
four by six index cards,
cut into cartoon-bone shapes.
These were for Cerberus
(Everyman's faithful dog),
who spends all his raucous leisure
scratching for that fleshless treasure.
(Cooper)[40]

CHAPTER 21

The Stones

When though the radiance which was once so bright
Be now forever taken from my sight,
Though nothing can bring back the hour
Of splendour in the grass, of glory in the flower;

—Wordsworth, "Ode on Intimations of Immortality from Recollections of Early Childhood"

The most bewildering feelings that Bob and I had were those of trying to reconcile our sadness at not having been present longer in each other's lives and at the same time not wanting to forfeit those parts of our past that we treasured. Wasting our time wishing for a past that could not have been was absurd. The best alternative was to tell as much of our stories to each other as we could. This would sometimes trouble Bob because he knew that there were gaps in his memory, especially of his childhood and youth. He seemed to have clear memories of his friends and their shenanigans, but family issues were the hardest for him to recall. I have always had a spotty memory; it is the recollections of my sister that trigger my memory of things that I have let slip from consciousness. Only rarely do I recall something that she has forgotten. I was fascinated by Bob's travels, and he was interested in how I had once helped build my own home and had been a part of a religious community that had a street ministry to the people living there. And while these were very different stories, there was a common ring to them. We were both children of middle-class families. Our mothers had been more educated than our fathers and had come from backgrounds diverse from those of their husbands.

We also found ourselves treasuring the detritus of each other's lives. After Bob's death, I found things in his underwear drawer that he had never seen me wear—things that had been worn long before I met him. He had held onto them because they connected him to a past that he had not been a part of, except that when he married me, he married everything that I was or ever had been—every success and every failure—and I had married the same in him. Sitting on my desk today are stones. One I picked up while standing on the shores of Galilee near a kibbutz where I was staying. The others are stones that Bob picked up through the years, both before and after we met. I've stacked them in cairns because I am standing at a crossroads in my now so puzzling life. Bob claimed that a rock was a rock until it was touched by the human hand and that, with human touch, it underwent an ontological shift. Something was conveyed to the rock, and it was converted to a stone, taking on some greater quality than it had had before. I found that idea so much at home in my soul—so real—and it was so Bobesque. As long as I knew him, he carried a stone in his pocket, and he wanted me to have one too. Standing in his office, he reached into his pocket one day and pulled out a stone that he had picked up from the ground at Camp Hartner in southern Louisiana when he had taken his turn as a young chaplain at a summer camp. That stone and one other had hung at his side, rubbing against coins and pocketknife for twenty years or more, and it had lost its rough edges. I named it "Louisiana." Recently when I was being taken in for yet another back surgery, I slipped Louisiana into Bailey's hand and said, "Don't lose this. It is more valuable to me than any diamond." I have treasured that stone and kept it with me since that day in Bob's office when it became mine.

Bob and I were both earth signs; some might say that we were earthy in our souls, that we were grounded in the soil and anything that came from it. I don't know much about that, but I do know that there was in us the ability for a connection to each other on that level. For one, we were forever scouring the earth for stones from the Frio River in Texas to the mountains above Steamboat Springs, Colorado. Bob specialized in river rocks, and I in fossils. We could not help ourselves; our eyes simply were fascinated by the formations of the earth and water.

When planning Bob's funeral, I went straight to the theme of stones, even put his beautiful poem "Patmos" on the back of the order of service. It seemed so right because over all those years of illness, misery, and loss, he had done exactly what the last line described. He had waited in faith until the "gone God" relented and waited until the angels came gliding down their mystical stairway to deliver him from all the suffering and to leave me, it seemed, with only what remains.

I wanted so much to get the funeral right, to sing the hymns Bob would have sung and read the scripture lessons he would have read. I did not resent having been left with the task; it felt good to have something to do, some purpose. I had forgotten how to do anything other than to take care of Bob; without that, my life seemed so directionless—so pointless. Over the years, I had asked Bob if we shouldn't make some plans for our funerals. He had no time for that. But on the day of his funeral, Patty spoke of how she would never forget the time that Bob showed up at her home, Prayer Book in hand, and said to her desperately ill husband, "George, let's plan your funeral." I thought, *that rascal, helping others plan their funerals and not planning his own.* He would just dismiss me, saying that I knew what he liked. But in the days after a death, the mind goes nearly blank. What was once so clear seems to get lost in some murk of disarray.

But in those horrible, unending days between Bob's death and the funeral, I made the choices about readings and music myself. Two hymns I absolutely knew Bob would have wanted, a third I wanted, but the fourth was a shot in the dark. Three months later, as I stood singing that same hymn in church one Sunday, I realized that the lyrics of that fourth hymn contained the title of Bob's doctoral dissertation, "Silent as Light." So many things like that would happen in the weeks and months ahead. It is now three years since Bob's passing, and I am still struck time and again by things that seem only he could have known to put in my path. If that is being crazy, I love being insane. I hope it never ends.

The Hebrew Testament lesson was one from Job. It had been our watchword, Bob's and mine, ever since my disastrous graduation day, "For thou shalt be like the stones of the field: and the wild beasts shall not harm thee" (Job 5.23).* That verse had been a source of great comfort to Bob and me, and it continues to be. It was to be read by a dear friend who is pastor of Faithful Temple Church, Ronny Young. He and his wife, Beverly, and their open-hearted congregation had tended to us with kindness and faith during our saddest days. If God had a voice, it would sound like Ronny's, and when that bleak day came, it seemed even deeper and fuller than usual. As I pondered these blessed words, I thought how true they had proven themselves to be; the wild beasts had not harmed us, not the beasts that sometimes break loose within the church, not the beasts of malicious gossip, not the beasts of illness, and now not the beast of death. We were safe, Bobby and I, just as we always had been, though we were not always aware of it.

The day of Bob's funeral, I had planned to wear a classic black crepe dress with pearls. Then at the last minute, standing there in the clothes closet, I felt the urge to wear the massive silver concha belt that Bob had bought for me on one of our trips to Santa Fe. I then put his Hopi cuff on my wrist. My skirt was suede, and my collar black fox. It was what Bob would have dressed me in—all things of the earth. I sat there in the pew so still, both within and without, numb maybe, but I think not. I heard Bruce's wonderfully magnolia-drenched voice coming from the back of the church, "I am the resurrection and the life ..." Now they were all coming into my view as they moved ponderously down the aisle and up the steps into the choir, Chris, Bishop Benfield of Arkansas, Dari bearing Bob's ashes with tears in his eyes, and all the others. The choir was so lovely. Then came the sound of Ronny's voice. I thought, *I am going to be all right. I am surrounded by those who love me. I am like a stone in the field.* "Louisiana" was in my hand.

* My translation

CHAPTER 22

The Fears

There are ways of doing this
String these lives on a singing thread
And draw it taut to raise our dead

—Robert Cooper, "Propers for an Unfixed Holy Day"[41]

I would soon be faced with my two greatest fears; the first one was from childhood, and the other more recently acquired. I was afraid of the dark, of being the last one asleep in a house emptied by the sleep of family members, and the latter was the fear of losing Bob. In the earliest days of our life together, he had stepped to the corner to turn on the ceiling fan. It had left an imprint of his long, narrow foot in the nap of the carpet. I could not vacuum it for fear that if the worst happened, it would be all that I had left of him. Rilke had written:

> Somewhere the flower of farewell blooms and scatters
> Ceaselessly; we draw in its pollen.
> Even in the coming winds we breathe farewell.*

I am not the first to make note of it. We are all passing away whether we are letting ourselves know it or not.

* AH-C translation.

Bob dreamed, and the dream became the thought that we were on a sinking ship and he wanted to be with Charlie and me, but we were apart. It was striking how often the metaphors of his dreams could find a literality in our life. We *were* on a sinking ship, and we *were* going to be separated. He wanted to talk often about the terrible dreams and also about the resurrection of the body. The first time this conversation of the latter took place was in his office at the seminary in our earliest days. He had asked if I believed in the resurrection of the body. I was hesitant to answer. He was the professor and I the student in a somewhat liberal seminary—or at least one that thought itself as such—but since I tend to tell the truth even when I shoot myself in the foot, I drew in a deep breath and said, "Yes." He let out this profound sigh of relief and said, "Good!" I was and am still convinced that we will be together again, and, moreover, we will recognize each other. I do believe that our lives are linked, that we will somehow make our way to each other. I believe that more now than ever in my life. I cannot know what form those bodies will take or how subtle they might become, but I do believe in the resurrection of the body—did then, do now.

A month to the hour after Bob's death, I was awakened in the early hours of the morning, just minutes before the exact second when he passed from my sight. What brought me to consciousness was the sound of his voice calling, "Annie! Annie!" It had the sound of urgency; I flew to my feet, calling out that I was coming. I was thinking that I had fallen asleep while waiting for my relief to arrive. I was horrified by my lapse. Also startled by all the commotion was Charlie, who rose up in the bed but did not follow. I came to reality and realized that Bob was gone from here, that his voice had come to me in some other way. Then I saw the hour. I went into the library, switched on the light, and began reading from my Prayer Book. When I next looked up, the time of his death had passed. I wandered back to my bed.

> Christ that my love were in my arms
> And I upon my bed. (Anonymous)

Life was becoming so fluid for me. I felt an evanescence that I had never experienced before. I felt as if I were living on the threshold between two worlds, and I belonged to neither. I felt like one who was passing away—unattached to life. Bob was as alive as he had ever been, and I was as dead as I ever would be. "The winds of farewell" were howling in my ears. The next months of grief were like a madness that I had never known before. I would awaken and be disappointed that my eyes had opened, that I had to face another day. I was not suicidal so much as that I could not imagine how one could go on living and be in such pain. I did not know what to do with myself. I was lovesick, and the loneliness of those times was palpable. I wanted someone who had known Bob in his prime who could sit with me for hours and reminisce about him. Interestingly enough, at least to me, was that my fears of being alone in the dark were gone. Oh, I missed him so, but that is not the same as being afraid.

Now, three years plus from his passing, I am more or less whole again. I can laugh, not just be sad and cry for the absence of the delight of the embodied man in my life. When I think of him, he is strong again. I don't dwell on his struggle to eat his supper or return to bed, as I once did; instead, I recall the man sitting in a lotus position on the floor, with me in his lap, my legs wrapped around his body, as he stood to answer the phone. I remember the strong man, the healthy man, the happy man. These memories are mine again, and such a source of enchantment they are. I am still in love with him and forever will be. I do long for him, and that "singing thread" that runs through him runs through me as well; it is drawn taut. For me, the dead live.

In my first dream of him after his death, we were standing in the hallway (an important location for Jungians), and we were having a serious conversation about something on which we had opposing positions. Suddenly he said, "You are right." And the dream ended. I woke, got out of bed, and stomped my way to the bathroom, shaking my fist at the Almighty. I wanted to know why in my first dream we had to be having an argument. Then suddenly I realized that Bob was well again. He could understand complex thoughts, reason, and then back down when he was wrong! That is health, not the sad loss of reasoning and fear of being found wrong that dementia brings. The dream also told me that I was recovering as well. I couldn't be myself until I let my mind and thoughts turn away from the wrenching soul pain of the dying days. I would now be giving birth to myself into a new life.

Bob taught me about stopping at the end of the day and enjoying a drink together. But with illness, Bob could no longer drink, and the late afternoons were the hardest to normalize. Even though those hours were those when we could be alone in the house together, they were also the hours when he often struggled with sundowners syndrome. It was a time of high anxiety. We would go into the kitchen and turn on all the lights to keep the shadows from disconcerting him. Then I would set my iPhone to the music most popular when we were falling in love. I would dance around him as he sat at the island, and I kept doing it until he was laughing and had forgotten the nightmare of his afternoon nap. I do not do these things today. I am not sure I will ever be able to fly that close to the bright light of those poignant memories again. My solution for that hour has been to work, and then at twilight or later, go into the library and say prayers. These quiet moments praying in that space that was his, that space of victory over suffering, has been a great source of comfort for me. I have continued our practice of beginning and ending each day with prayer. It brings him nearer to me, or perhaps it is the other way around. Either way, we stand in each other's presence before the throne of grace.

We have come a long way. There were the hours of love, struggle, physical pain, defeat, success, glorious hours of work—hard work—fear, complete bliss, hours of each other, disbelief that we were—despite all—together, glorious blessings, sorrow, grief, pleasure, beauty, cherished friendships, love of parishioners, adoration of each other, loss of parents, pleasure in children and the delight of grandchildren, encouragement to press on, respect, discoveries, laughter, and always love, love unlike we had ever known—what glorious times—and then illness and death. Those good times were to be banked against the hard times when we would have to draw on them, until the goodness returned and we could be deeply in love again. There were passion-filled years of bliss followed by the years of troubled, struggling love that was tempered by the onset of dementia, and then a Divine, spirit-driven, profound love born of horrible tribulation and shared sorrow. This is the love that endures. All of this was made all the more intense by the certain knowledge that death lay ahead. One of us would go and leave the other behind. At night, when I lie in my "big, lonely bed" I ask myself how I have come to this place, and the answer always comes back—love called, and love answered. There is no greater motivation and no greater reward than love.

CHAPTER 23

The Watch, The Note, and The Fish Crows

Out of Sight? What of that?
See the Bird—reach it!
Curve by Curve—Sweep by Sweep
Round the Steep Air—

—Emily Dickinson, "Out of Sight What of That?"

Nine of the most blissful years of my life were spent with Bob in our condo on the west coast of Florida, where we could decompress from work that was both demanding and important in, what Bob has described as, an unspectacular way. From our south windows, we looked down the intercoastal waterway toward St. Petersburg, and the west windows let out onto a view that went beyond the unpopulated barrier island and on to the Gulf of Mexico. It was a beautiful place from which we could watch the evening ritual of the fish crows that would fly out in great swarms toward these islands, then swoop back inland again, each time gathering greater numbers of their flock until finally, before the sun set, they would settle in the distant palm trees until morning. In all, it was a visual paradise that brought healing to our exhausted bodies and psyches.

Farther down the intercoastal in St. Petersburg was the Dali Museum where Bob and I went often. On one visit, we saw the painting done by Dali in 1931 to which he had given the name *The Persistence of Memory.* Most of us are familiar with this piece; it is the one in which there are faces of clocks that seem to be melting away—time being distorted, pulled downward and flattening out as if it were made of wax and therefore vulnerable to the heat of time—pliable time that creeps when we are young or in pain or grieving and flies when we are old or happy or in love. It is disorienting to look at this painting, haunting even. Bob had been intrigued by it, and, I suppose, I had been too, though I had a lower tolerance than he did for things like that. The painting unsettles me. I could not look at it long before I had to glance away. But I would find myself coming back to it—snatching another look. I had had the same reaction to it as a young art student seeing reproductions of it in textbooks or flashed up on screens before our class, but the connection between time and memory or the distortion of memory with time was lost on me when I was young. My reaction then had been purely visceral; I was a youth and invulnerable to the blows of time, I thought. But if it is true that youth finds itself invulnerable, why had it haunted me so—and for all these years? Why had it left me with such dis-ease? Does the body know what reason cannot? I think it must. Or perhaps Rilke was right when he claimed that our destiny rises up from within us rather than coming at us from some distance.

Soon after viewing the Dali, I found a watch that had on its face a detail reproduced from that painting, and because Bob liked the painting so much, I bought the watch. Soon it was on Bob's wrist. It was far from being among the finer watches that I gave him, yet after his death, when I began sorting through all of them, I found that the Dali was the one that showed the greatest wear. To look at it was painful. Time and memory linked together melting down to naught. What a horrible prophecy it had been.

The inexplicable thing is that I took the watch to my jeweler to see if he could get it running again. After careful examination, more than it deserved, he kindly said that if I had my heart set on it, he could try to get it going again, but the battery had sprung a leak, and the repairs would likely be more than the watch had cost new. Then there would still have to be a new band that would fit my wrist. I was confused by myself. I really didn't want the watch. I wanted Bob. I must have looked downcast because this kind man beckoned me behind the counter and to his workbench. He said, "Let me help you throw it away." He put it in one of those small tan envelopes and wrapped the string around the paper button to secure it. Then he handed the sad bundle to me and pointed me toward his trash can where it sank beneath the paper scraps like a body at sea. I couldn't speak; I just gave him one of those feeble waves and hoped that it said, "Thank you. Goodbye. You must be one of the kindest men I have ever met. And I must get out of here before I become completely undone." Back in the car, I was asking myself why everything had become a metaphor. In every little loss, I was seeing the truest loss of all, again and again. I was being overtaken by pain. I was almost paralyzed by longing. That was early on, and I had not given myself much time to mend at all. I was so impatient with myself; I was so broken.

When I first met Bob, he did not wear a watch but carried a small alarm clock with him to class. For the remainder of time, he could do rather well at estimating the time. He simply had lived his life for so long in hourly increments that he had learned to tell time instinctively. One day, he admired a wristwatch he saw in the *New York Times* and said, somewhat wistfully, that he had once worn a watch. That's all it took for me to jump into action; his watches began arriving. I like watches. I must have some fascination with that old goat of *Kronos* ticking his rhythm into me. As Bob grew more and more disoriented, even the digital clocks with the exact time of day and week could not keep him clear about whether it was morning or evening. But still he wanted to be surrounded by clocks. Clocks, watches, time, memory—all melting away before his eyes and he watching but only faintly able to see time was passing by, as batteries leaked and bands cracked. Now that he is gone, his love lingers. I am surrounded by it every moment of the day. It fills my sleep, and it makes life possible. Without it, I could not have endured his loss.

Just days before the second Christmas after Bob's passing from our sight, a Christmas that I felt compelled to spend alone, I picked up a Bible that I had not used in almost thirty years. Drifting out of the pages came a note written in Bob's hand, a note of which I have only the vaguest memory of receiving.

Ann Precious—

I had to leave early—

I left a prayer—

Love you, B

Yes, Bobby, you had to leave early, but please don't forget the way of the fish crows and double back for me. See me home safely before night falls.

Precious-dog-Charlie

Bob on the shores of Inks Lake

Ann and Bob on the evening of their wedding.

ENDNOTES

1 e. e. cummings, "i carry your heart within me," *E. E. Cummings Complete Poems 1904—1962,* #92, ed. George J. Firmage (New York: Liveright Publishing Corporation, 1991), 766.
2 Rainer Maria Rilke, "Turning Point," *The Selected Poems of Rainer Maria Rilke,* ed. and trans. Edward Snow (New York: Random House, 1982), 132–135.
3 Robert Cooper, "January," *Anglican Theological Review* 71, no. 4 (1989): 427.
4 O. C. Edwards, in a letter written for the roast (1990).
5 William Pregnall, in a letter for the roast (2990).
6 Cooper, "The Immanent John Leadmine," unpublished (1984).
7 Bruce McMillan, letter written for a roast of Robert M. Cooper (1990).
8 Søren Kierkegaard, *Either/Or Vol I,* ed. and trans. Howard V. Wong and Edna H. Hong (Princeton: Princeton University Press, 1987), 30.
9 Robert Cooper, "Childhood's Nocturnal Journey," unpublished, undated.
10 Dale Coleman, The Rev., in a note of condolence (2014).
11 Cooper, "In Memoriam: Elmer Gantry," seemingly unpublished (ca. 1965).
12 Cooper, "A House in the Zodiac," *Anglican Theological Review* 68, no. 2 (1986): 139.
13 Cooper, "St. Bruno," *Ratherview* (February 1982): 11.
14 Alfred North Whitehead, "Process and Reality: An Essay in Cosmology," in *Process and Reality: Corrected Edition,* ed. David R. Griffin and Donald W. Sherburne (New York: The Free Press, 1978), 338.
15 Cooper, "You Had Said," seemingly unpublished (ca 1985).
16 Cooper, "There Are Too Damned Many Ghosts Now," seemingly unpublished, undated.
17 Robert M. Cooper, "The Spirite Searcheth the Botome of Goddess Secrets," *Engaging the Spirit,* ed. Robert B. Slocum, 57–71 (New York: Church Publishing, 2001), 71.
18 Robert Cooper, "Patmos," *The Classical Outlook,* fall issue (1997): 2.
19 Cooper, "A Red Panther for Rembrandt Bugati," seemingly unpublished, ca 1985.
20 Steve Gruman, in a letter written for a roast (January 19, 1985).

21 Robert Cooper, "Laying on of Hands," *The Tennessee Churchman* 8, no. 4 (1971): 1.
22 Cooper, untitled and dated (ca. 1985).
23 Cooper, "Pangaea," *Psychological Perspectives* 38, winter issue (1998–1999): 68.
24 Linda Ori, "! The Frog Prince," retrieved from poemhunter.com, 2007.
25 Robert Cooper, "... But for Death," *Anglican Theological Review* 77, no. 2 (1999): 211.
26 Cooper, "Looms of Our Mothers," *Odd Angles of Heaven: Contemporary Poetry by People of Faith*, ed. David Craig, Janet McCann (College Station, TX: Department of English, Texas A&M University, 1998): 68.
27 Cooper, "Gone," unpublished and undated.
28 Cooper, "Desert," *Anglican Theological Review* 62, no. 2 (1980): 170.
29 Cooper, "Divorce," unpublished (ca. 1975).
30 Cooper, "The Panther," *The Classical Outlook*, fall issue (1997): 3.
31 Cooper, "Thinking About Her Again," unpublished (spring, 1985).
32 Cooper, untitled, undated.
33 Cooper, "Praise to the Mole (Homage to Kafka)," *Anglican Theological Review* 54, no. 4 (1972): 343.
34 Cooper, "And Ships An Ocean," *Periplum: An Anthology of Austin Poets*, ed. John Herndon (Austin: Open Theatre Publishers, 1987), 24.
35 Cooper, a note left on the kitchen counter, April 1991.
36 Cooper, "You Know Why This is Yours," unpublished (1995).
37 Cooper, "AH'S," unpublished poem (ca. 1985).
38 Cooper. "Father it is Your Birthday," *Old Hickory Revie* 2, no. 2 (fall 1970): 42.
39 Cooper, "Say When the Dying is Done," print by permission in *Imagination and Ministry* written by Urban T. Holmes (New York: Seabury Press, 1976), 144.
40 Cooper, "Everything Died Today," *The Christian Century; An Ecumenical Weekly* 89, no. 28 (August 1972): 792.
41 Cooper, "Propers for an Unfixed Holy Day," *The Living Church* 182, no. 4 (January 25, 1981): 2.

CPSIA information can be obtained
at www.ICGtesting.com
Printed in the USA
LVHW110820191119
637818LV00007B/206/P